Praise for *The I*

What a beautiful collection of meditations on the closeness of Jesus amidst our anxiety! With tenderness and vulnerability, Tessa invites readers who feel weary and worn down by darkness and despair to come find rest for their souls in Jesus.

ASHERITAH CIUCIU, national speaker, host of the *Prayers of Rest* podcast, and author of many books, including *Full, Prayers of Rest,* and *Unwrapping the Names of Jesus*

Tessa has a way of validating feelings of anxiety, fear, and doubt while offering encouragement no matter our circumstances. She doesn't wrap readers' experiences into a tidy bow, but instead allows for life's unexpected twists, all while offering the hope of Christ. Each devotional bears a richness and wisdom that comes only from personal experience. Tessa journeys alongside readers as a trusted friend who recognizes our collective pain, sharing her experiences openly and vulnerably, and reminding us to cling to Jesus in all seasons of life.

KENDRA ROEHL, speaker and author of several devotionals, including *The One Year Daily Acts of Gratitude Devotional: 365 Inspirations to Encourage a Life of Thankfulness,* and co-creator of the online community TheRuthExperience.com

In a world that pulls at us every moment, stilling our soul to rest in the presence of Jesus can feel impossible. In this beautiful devotional, you'll find peace for your racing mind and hope for your weary heart. *The Rested Soul* belongs on every nightstand or coffee table reminding you that you never go through life alone. Jesus knows, He cares, and He is carrying you.

ERICA WIGGENHORN, Bible teacher, national speaker, and author of women's Bible studies and *Letting God Be Enough: Why Striving Keeps You Stuck and How Surrender Sets You Free*

Do you need rest from the tensions and traumas of life? You've come to the right place! Tessa Afshar offers a beautiful invitation to experience the rest Christ promises. If the stresses and strains of life have left you weary, keep this devotional close. You'll be sure to return to it often whenever anxiety threatens to overwhelm. I highly recommend this devotional for every anxious soul!

BECKY HARLING, coach, conference speaker, and author of *Psalms for the Anxious Heart* and *Cultivating Deeper Connections in a Lonely World*

This devotional is not like any other. It touches you deep in your soul and changes you. I love the efficient and effective format that fits perfectly into busy schedules. Each day has a powerful verse, words of experience, wisdom from Tessa, intentional questions to linger on, guided prayer, and ends with an oasis and rest that tangibly covers you. You cannot help but take that oasis with you the rest of the day. God used this valuable devotional in my life, and I believe He will do the same for anyone who reads it!

JENNIFER A. CHAPMAN, founder and president, Mastering Motherhood

the Rested Soul

30 Meditations to Quiet Your Heart

Tessa Afshar

Moody Publishers

CHICAGO

© 2024 by
TESSA AFSHAR

All rights reserved. No part of this book including photographs may be reproduced in any form without permission in writing from the publisher, except in the case of brief quotations embodied in critical articles or reviews.

Unless otherwise marked, Scripture quotations are from the ESV® Bible (The Holy Bible, English Standard Version®), © 2001 by Crossway, a publishing ministry of Good News Publishers. Used by permission. All rights reserved. The ESV text may not be quoted in any publication made available to the public by a Creative Commons license. The ESV may not be translated in whole or in part into any other language.

Scripture quotations marked (NIV) are taken from the Holy Bible, New International Version®, NIV®. Copyright © 1973, 1978, 1984, 2011 by Biblica, Inc.™ Used by permission of Zondervan. All rights reserved worldwide. www.zondervan.com The "NIV" and "New International Version" are trademarks registered in the United States Patent and Trademark Office by Biblica, Inc.™

Scripture quotations marked (NLT) are taken from the *Holy Bible*, New Living Translation, copyright ©1996, 2004, 2015 by Tyndale House Foundation. Used by permission of Tyndale House Publishers, Carol Stream, Illinois 60188. All rights reserved.

Portions of a few of these stories have appeared in a different form in some of the author's other writings.

Published in association with Books & Such Literary Management, www.booksandsuch.com.

Edited by Pamela Joy Pugh
Interior design: Puckett Smartt
Cover design: Erik M. Peterson
Cover photo of beach and all interior photos courtesy of Tessa Afshar
Cover graphic of paper copyright © 2023 by Custom Scene/Adobe Stock (509911165). All rights reserved.
Author photo: Emilie Haney at EAHCreative.com
Photos have been reprinted with permission for the exclusive and express use in this publication.

Library of Congress Cataloging-in-Publication Data

Names: Afshar, Tessa, author.
Title: The rested soul : 30 meditations to quiet your heart / Tessa Afshar.
Description: Chicago : Moody Publishers, [2024] | Includes bibliographical
   references. | Summary: "True shalom for an anxiety-ridden world. Tessa
   brings you on a journey that cultivates a rested soul. Her beautiful
   meditations create an oasis of calm when powerful storms of anxiety
   assail you. She brings you into your hope-filled, joy-infused life in
   Jesus. In Him, we find The Rested Soul"-- Provided by publisher.
Identifiers: LCCN 2023039257 (print) | LCCN 2023039258 (ebook) | ISBN
   9780802431172 (paperback) | ISBN 9780802473318 (ebook)
Subjects: LCSH: Calmness. | Meditations. | Christian life. |
   Spirituality--Christianity. | BISAC: RELIGION / Christian Living /
   Devotional | RELIGION / Christian Living / Women's Interests
Classification: LCC BF575.C35 A343 2024 (print) | LCC BF575.C35 (ebook) |
   DDC 242/.4--dc23/eng/20231122
LC record available at https://lccn.loc.gov/2023039257
LC ebook record available at https://lccn.loc.gov/2023039258

Originally delivered by fleets of horse-drawn wagons, the affordable paperbacks from D. L. Moody's publishing house resourced the church and served everyday people. Now, after more than 125 years of publishing and ministry, Moody Publishers' mission remains the same—even if our delivery systems have changed a bit. For more information on other books (and resources) created from a biblical perspective, go to www.moodypublishers.com or write to:

Moody Publishers
820 N. LaSalle Boulevard
Chicago, IL 60610

1 3 5 7 9 10 8 6 4 2

Printed in the United States of America

For my father who taught me joy.

I still miss you every day.

Contents

INTRODUCTION

My Personal Battle 9

Devotional Overview 12

Photography 14

MEDITATIONS

You Are Not Alone 17

You Can Endure 21

Enlarge Your Hope 27

Your Balm 31

God's "Such a Time as This" 35

Peace Like a River 41

Your Anchor Point 45

Your Wonderful Counselor 51

Your Breakthrough 57

Hold Fast 61

The Father Is with Me 67

Small Thing 71

Not Forsaken 75

Your New Strength 81

Set Aside 87

Aligned with the Spirit 93

The Lord Is My Peace 99

A Soft Heart 105

You Can Withstand the Attack 109

Your Fortress 115

You Are Favored 121

Little by Little 125

An Honest Scale 131

Take Back That Throne 137

The Consolation of God's Glory 143

Your Rescue 149

Your Rest 155

Contending for Contentment 161

Victory Over Discouragement and Pain 167

Life Is Beautiful 171

Acknowledgments 177

Introduction

MY PERSONAL BATTLE

Twenty years ago, my life fell apart.

For several years, I had been working long hours, pushing myself beyond my natural strength, shouldering pressures that I had not been designed to carry.

Sometimes, for short seasons, God allows us to go through intense periods of labor, toiling past the edge of what our soul and body can bear. But these are exceptions. They are not meant to become a way of life. The Bible's patterns of work are carefully interrupted by regular seasons of rest, by festivals of worship and spiritual renewal. God considers true rest so important to our being that He made it one of His central commandments.

My choices did not reflect this biblical balance.

Instead, my short season of stress turned into a way of life. Year after year, I pushed myself beyond my endurance until, finally, I experienced a terrifying burnout. For a whole month, I could not work, or pray, or accomplish anything. At the end of that month, when I returned to work, I had no idea if I could get through the first hour, let alone the whole week or year.

The unrelenting fatigue opened the door to a more insidious force: anxiety.

I began to feel anxious, at first about specific things. A deadly parade of *what-ifs* that attacked me relentlessly. *What if I never improved? What if I couldn't work? What if this was the rest of my life? What if I couldn't pay the mortgage?*

Because these thoughts were so persistent, they dug a trench into my psyche. Anxiety became a way of life. Even when I wasn't thinking of any scary possibilities, I felt anxious. Everything sparked a fire of stress: work, travel, people. All of life had become overwhelming.

I sought the right help, both medical and spiritual. I wished I could say that I overcame the snare of anxiety with several powerful prayers, a few days of fasting, and a loud hallelujah. But that was not my experience. It took about two-and-a-half years to tame this debilitating enemy.

At the end of this terrifying season, I was surprised to discover that my greatest blessing was not the fact that I experienced relief from anxiety, although that was wonderful! But to my astonishment, I actually found something even better. As we are promised in the book of Romans, I discovered that I emerged from my drawn-out battle more than a conqueror (Rom. 8:37). I walked out of that dark valley with an irreplaceable treasure.

I found a deeper attachment to Jesus.

I discovered an intimacy with God that became the spine of my life. I learned to anchor my soul in the eternal in such a way that I stopped being tossed up and down with every wave of circumstance. In the process, God graciously removed several deep-seated blocks to His work in my life.

God sometimes heals us outright. He utterly banishes the thing that torments us. At other times, He allows a fragility to remain. A part of your soul where you will always need to lean on Him extra hard.

A couple of decades after my initial struggle with anxiety, the pandemic hit. During that time, my family experienced some lingering health issues. Anxiety managed to get its claws into me again. But I noticed it was different this time. It didn't go all the way to my core the way it had in the first round. It was as if I had an anxiety-proof foundation. Even though my mind grappled with the general unease that comes from catastrophic thinking, I wasn't shaken at my core.

I felt anxiety's sting. But I wasn't overcome by it.

I have found, even though I remain at some level vulnerable to anxiety, it no longer enslaves me. It doesn't own me. I walk in a new freedom even when I experience its sharp, little fangs.

God has imparted a steadfast security to me that I had not known before my original battle. It's as if that struggle broke an invisible chain that I did not know I wore.

Jesus taught my soul to be quieted through the battle.

I don't know what your valley is. Maybe, like me, you are struggling with anxiety. Maybe the monster that hounds you is discouragement, or burnout, or a loss of hope for your future. Whatever your struggle, I want you to know there is a way through this.

I have attempted to capture in this book some of the lessons of my hard years to help you begin the process of breaking your own chains.

I hope these meditations will quiet your heart and inspire you to remove the obstacles that may be blocking the rest that God wants for your soul. I pray that in the pages of these devotions you will find a peaceful oasis in the midst of your wilderness.

DEVOTIONAL OVERVIEW

I want to take you to a deep place with God because that is where you will find rest for your soul. At the same time, I have tried to keep each entry simple, so that if you are having a hard time focusing, your mind will not be overwhelmed by the message.

I begin each meditation with Scripture. The devotional includes a personal anecdote followed by the core message. Some of the messages remind you of important truths that your soul needs in order to experience rest. Others help you identify and remove obstacles that block God's peace. I also identify specific words and verses that can act as a spiritual anchor for your heart, providing a quick sense of security and stability.

Following each devotional, you are invited to take time to *Linger*. This is an opportunity to sit in the Lord's presence and ask yourself a significant question or two. Have you believed a particular lie? Can you trust in this specific promise for your life? These kinds of questions help you to spend guided time unearthing what is going on in your soul.

Following your inward time of quiet, you will find a short *Prayer*. Though simple, these prayers go after big things. They give God permission to move. They lean hard into Jesus.

The next section is called *Oasis,* and it can play an important part in your journey to rest. I have written some prompts based on Scripture. Here, you can speak to Jesus. But I especially encourage you to listen for His voice as prompted by these verses. What does He want you to internalize about His promise? How does He want you to lean more deeply into Him here?

Thomas à Kempis wrote, "Blessed is that man who hears Jesus speaking in his soul, and who takes from His mouth some word of comfort. Blessed are those ears which hear the secret whisperings of Jesus, and give no heed to the deceitful whisperings of this world."[1] The more you can hear from Jesus, the less the enemy's whispers have power over you.

Each meditation ends with a segment called *Rest.* Here you say a final prayer and choose to rest in a specific biblical promise for that day.

You can go through these meditations at your own pace. You may read them all in one sitting, or you might just get through one verse and look at a picture that day. Wherever you are, this book is for you. You get to use it at your pace.

---

1. Thomas à Kempis, *The Imitation of Christ* (New York: Doubleday, 1989), 103.

PHOTOGRAPHY

I hope the beautiful photos in this book minister peace to your heart. My husband took every single picture, but you will not find his name anywhere in this devotional. He purposely requested this omission in order to protect me.

Because I was born in the Middle East and converted to Christianity as an adult, we try to add what security measures we can to what has become a somewhat public life. I write under my maiden name. We don't share my married name, which adds an extra layer of protection to my daily life. That's why my husband gave up the credit for his photography.

Just know that a kind, gentle man is behind these photographs. It is his hope that you will be blessed by them.

Meditations

You Are Not Alone

My soul is crushed with grief.

MARK 14:34 NLT

When my father was in his fifties, he lived through a bloody revolution in the Middle East. Overnight his secure, comfortable world was gone. He watched as his friends were arrested and even put to death. His own life seemed to hang in the balance. After decades of hard work as a physician, he lost his life savings as banks simply collapsed.

Without warning, everything he knew had turned upside down. All this loss proved too much. For two years, anxiety devoured his mind. Eventually, he managed to rebuild a new life, which ultimately led him to faith in Christ.

Twenty-five years later, I fell into my own dark well as I struggled with burnout. Anxiety became my daily companion, sometimes a low hum, sometimes a debilitating roar.

One day as I sat across from my father, I tried to explain my frustration with my inability to reason myself into well-being.

"I can't argue with these irrational feelings. I can't talk myself out of them. I can't fix them."

My father looked at me, his eyes welling up with compassion. He didn't give me any advice. He didn't come up with a plan of action. He just whispered, "I know. I know."

In the long months it took for me to inch my way toward recovery, I have always thought of that as the most helpful moment of my journey. It wasn't an answer or a cure. It was simply the loving empathy of a man who had lived through a similar ache and made it to the other side to find peace.

This book hinges on that reality: beloved, you are not alone.

I know.

More importantly, other women and men who loved God have walked

this path and emerged on the other side to find rest for their souls. David, who said, "I am feeble and crushed; I groan because of the tumult of my heart," understands your struggle (Ps. 38:8). Naomi, who felt exceedingly bitter with loss and grief, gets your dark sorrow. They've been there.

Most powerful of all, Jesus, who said, "My soul is crushed with grief to the point of death" (Mark 14:34 NLT), knows the burden of suffering and sorrow that you carry. They know.

You are not alone.

And peace awaits on the other side of this journey. There is an end to this travail. Your soul will be quieted. Your heart can find rest.

Settle in that hope.

Your first step is to remember you are not alone. Jesus is with you. He knows.

LINGER

Have I been feeling all alone in my pain?

PRAYER

God, I feel overwhelmed. Help me cling to You in this wilderness. Help me know You cling to *me* through every hard step. Remind me that I'm not alone. Remind me there will be an end. Holy Spirit, help me find peace before I have understanding.

OASIS

Jesus, You understand my weakness. You sympathize with it. Show me how Your companionship in the midst of this struggle is enough to see me through. ~ Hebrews 4:15

REST

From the end of the earth I call to you
when my heart is faint.
Lead me to the rock that is higher than I.

PSALM 61:2

Jesus, I will rest in the knowledge that You are my safe place. You are the rock that stands higher than the swelling waves of my emotions.

You Can Endure

Here is a call for the endurance and faith of the saints.

REVELATION 13:10

My husband loves sunflowers. As novice gardeners, we decided to grow several varieties in our small yard. Because we live in the cold climate of New England, we grew the seedlings indoors before transferring them outside. A lot of the seeds never germinated. Having lost over half, every single seedling became precious to us by the time we planted them in the yard.

One of the plants seemed to be doing well until a squirrel beheaded it so that only the two seed leaves remained, and even they were yellowed and more dead than alive. I was certain it could not grow back from that assault. But that plucky thing struggled, and a couple of other leaves finally shot out, followed by a couple more. It was a valiant effort. Hubby and I watched in wonder as it proved us wrong in all our predictions of doom and gloom.

Then some kind of disease attacked the delicate leaves and they started turning brown. We sprayed them with organic pest-control oil though we had little hope. To our amazement, the sunflower started to grow again, shooting out healthy green leaves.

To our dismay, a mysterious pest started eating our plant. It was so small and damaged by this time that we were sure it couldn't get past this new assault.

But it did.

I was starting to love this plant. Nearby, other sunflowers were growing tall and producing massive blooms that drew the praise of neighbors. Even the goldfinches loved to rest in the enormous disks of their flowers.

But this little plant, which hadn't even had a chance to bloom, stole my heart. That feisty sunflower became the glory of our garden.

Its beauty wasn't in its perfection or productivity. We didn't care that it was slower than the other plants. What we loved was that our fragile sunflower held on.

Maybe right now you feel like that broken sunflower. Maybe in comparison to those around you, you feel like a failure. You feel like you have nothing but pain to show for your life.

When you are crushed by one trauma after another, you may feel like you are not worthy. But God doesn't see your life like that. You are the glory of His garden. Sometimes, our glory comes from a crushed life. A difficult life, well-lived.

Right now, your job is to hang on. To get up again and again. To hold on to Jesus and not let go.

Right now is not the end of your story.

Just as all those attacks weren't the end of our sunflower. Eventually, our plant grew sturdy, shooting out healthy stalks and leaves. Every jaw dropped as its multiple blossoms opened and matured. We had long since forgotten the variety of sunflower we had planted. So those flowers took us by surprise. The only Teddy Bear variety growing in our yard produced breathtaking golden yellow fluffy blooms. We couldn't stop staring at those gorgeous, Van Gogh-worthy flowers and sigh with pleasure. After a long, hard battle, they had managed to fulfill our best hopes and plans for them.

You may feel so caught up in this present pain that you have forgotten

the beauty God has planted in you. Let me tell you: you are a marvel of God's creation! Your beauty will be fully revealed in God's time.

God's kingdom intentions for your life are mighty even if they don't translate into worldly success.

As you wait in the midst of this emotional travail, your glory shines for those who have eyes to see. Right now, when I talk to Jesus about you, I whisper, "The glory of Your garden."

~~~~~~~~~~~~~~~~~~~~~~~~~~~~~~~~

LINGER

Is part of me ready to give up?

Do I really believe that God's glory will be seen upon my life?

~ Isaiah 60:2

PRAYER

Father, help me hold on. Help me endure. Help me not give in to discouragement or despair. Jesus, I choose to trust You even though I am running out of strength. Let others see Your glory upon my life in spite of my brokenness. Grant that my life will one day become beautifully fruitful.

OASIS

Jesus, do You want to give me strength to rise again and again?

~ Proverbs 24:16

Jesus, will You strengthen me when I am faint and weary?

~ Isaiah 40:29–31

REST

Can anything ever separate us from Christ's love? Does it mean he no longer loves us if we have trouble or calamity, or are persecuted, or hungry, or destitute, or in danger, or threatened with death?

ROMANS 8:35 NLT

Jesus, I choose to rest in Your love. Help me be quieted in the knowledge that none of this present trouble can diminish the power of Your love at work in my life.

Enlarge Your Hope

"Enlarge the place of your tent,
And let the curtains of your habitations be stretched out;
Do not hold back; lengthen your cords
and strengthen your stakes."

ISAIAH 54:2

At some point in my long battle with anxiety, I began to wonder if my future was ruined. There were weeks when my hope for restoration shriveled. Sometimes, the enemy whispered that I was now unworthy. And I believed him.

Maybe you feel that way. Maybe you feel like your future is now damaged. That you are yourself damaged. If somewhere in your deepest heart you have come to the conclusion that you are doomed to remain in this pit, small and vulnerable for the rest of your life, listen to Isaiah's words:

Enlarge the place of your tent!

Isaiah said these words to Judah when the kingdom was in a state of helpless captivity. When God's people were at their most broken. When they felt utterly vanquished.

It is one of the most counterintuitive promises of God to His people. In the midst of their shattered and small lives, He promised them an increase.

Don't measure your future by this present experience, Isaiah was promising. Get ready to grow. Get ready to be enlarged. Get ready to bear fruit.

The inference of the whole passage is that Israel will be more than it was before. You and I need to receive this promise for our own lives.

This message is as true for you as it was for captive Judah.

How can I make this claim? Because years before this prophecy, Isaiah made another prediction about the coming Messiah. This prediction was for all who belong to that Messiah, including you and me: "Of the increase of his government and of peace there will be no end" (Isa. 9:7).

Did you notice the word *increase* in that promise? When you belong to Jesus, His kingdom is steadily increasing within you.

Like captive Israel you are invited to enlarge your expectations of God's kingdom within you because you belong to the Prince of Peace.

Right now, in this dark place, a part of you is being enlarged. Strengthened to carry the weight of the increase that God has for you. Even though you are going through a diminished season, you can trust that God is laying a foundation in that valley for a greater glory in your life.

In every life, this will work out differently. But my friend, your spirit is increasing in this dark valley. When you emerge from it, you may still feel vulnerable. You may feel fragile. But there will be an increase in you that has been wrought by the Spirit of God.

It may be an increase in understanding. In healing. In knowledge. In patience. In grace. In godliness. You may find an increase in opportunities, in joy, in influence.

God is increasing His influence in you in order to increase His influence through you.

One thing you can bank on: Jesus plans to enlarge your life by governing it through this hard season. So invite Him to take over the full government of your heart during this time. Give Him permission to have His way. Whatever your increase may look like, you will be able to bless others with it. In this way, this present darkness, this fang of anxiety, will also be the servant of Christ. You can enlarge your hope without fearing disappointment.

~~~~~~

LINGER

Have I believed that I am damaged goods, and not as good as everyone else?
Can I really believe that God plans an enlarged life for me?

PRAYER

Jesus, I invite You to increase in me and increase me. Forgive me for putting blocks in Your path. Forgive me for believing that I am worth less than others. Help me enlarge the place of my tent in my spirit. Help me expect more from You. More healing, more understanding, more grace, more influence. I welcome You to strengthen my spirit that I may one day bear the weight of all the increase You have in store for me. I invite You to take over the government of my life.

OASIS

Jesus, do You really want to increase Your kingdom in me?

~ Isaiah 9:7

REST

Of the increase of his government and of peace there will be no end.

ISAIAH 9:7

Jesus, I rest knowing that You plan to increase Your peace in me.

Your Balm

Is there no balm in Gilead?
Is there no physician there?
Why then has the health of the daughter of my people
not been restored?

JEREMIAH 8:22

Last year, my friend had to have eye surgery. In preparation for the procedure, the surgeon explained that she needed to have eye drops custom-made for her. Not an over-the-counter medication. But drops, he explained, that would be derived from her own blood!

The resultant fluid would provide the greatest healing balm for her wounded eyes post-surgery. Science could not match what her own blood could provide.

I love this image. It reminds me of the Balm of Gilead (Jer. 8:22). Gilead was a region around the river Jabbok to the north of the Dead Sea. This area was famous for producing a medicinal substance that had widespread therapeutic usage. In Jeremiah, as God enumerates the heartbreaking sins and incurable wounds of His people, He cries out, "Is there no balm in Gilead?"

It's an aching question. Is there no remedy? No cure? But God answers His own question as only He can. He answers it on the cross. Yes! There is a balm to heal the incurable wound of God's children. It is a balm made from blood, just like my friend's eye drops.

Only you and I don't have what it takes to create the balm we need for ourselves. Our own blood is too tainted.

We are too broken. Too fallen.

Sometimes, when life is hard, when discouragement is roaring at the door, this is where we get stuck. In the brokenness. In the helplessness. In the insufficiency of our humanity.

We get stuck living as if there is no Balm in Gilead.

We live as if the Son of God never emptied Himself into the womb of Mary. We forget that He chose to lay down His glory. He left behind His majesty and took up forty-six DNA molecules that made up three billion nucleotide pairs sequenced to make Him fully human. He became a kinsman in order to become our Redeemer.

A man who shed tears. Who hurt. Who bled. Blood that was fully divine and fully human. Blood that could cover our sins and release us from the dominion of death.

Blood that provides healing for our wounds.

When I get wrangled into a dark corner by discouragement or weariness, I tend to forget this about Jesus. Forget the sheer power of His blood that covers my life. My brain remembers it. I have sat through too many Bible studies to forget that much. But my heart loses sight of it.

My heart forgets there is a Balm in Gilead.

Maybe that's where you find yourself. Maybe you are sinking into discouragement today. Maybe self-pity has wrestled you to the ground. Maybe anxiety has taken a chunk out of you.

There is a phrase that the disciples pick up from Jesus and use multiple times. These words pour strength into me every time I read them:

"Take heart."

Jesus says "take heart" to the woman with the issue of blood (Matt. 9:22); to the paralytic (Matt. 9:2); to the disciples (Matt. 14:27). In different situations, whether facing fear, discouragement, or the power of sin, Jesus whispers, "Take heart."

Coming from Jesus, this isn't empty comfort. To the part of you that feels constant anxiety, the part of you that has become hypervigilant and cannot rest, Jesus whispers: "Take heart."

Take heart, beloved. Whatever your circumstances, I want you to remember this: the blood of Jesus is more powerful. His sacrifice on the cross releases the healing of heaven into our lives. Take heart.

LINGER

Do I truly believe that Jesus is the Balm of Gilead in *my* life?

PRAYER

Lord Jesus, my Balm of Gilead, I offer You my wounded heart. I give You my bruises, my scars, my fears, my brokenness. Jesus, cover me with Your holy blood. Heal me. Help me take heart.

OASIS

Jesus, will You help me take heart in the midst of my fears?
~ Matthew 14:27

REST

But he was pierced for our transgressions,
He was crushed for our iniquities;
The punishment that brought us peace was on him,
And by his wounds we are healed.

ISAIAH 53:5 NIV

Lord, I rest in Your peace. The peace You purchased for me on the cross. By Your wounds I am healed.

God's "Such a Time as This"

"And who knows but that you have come to your royal position for such a time as this?"

ESTHER 4:14 NIV

As I struggled with lingering anxiety that followed on the heels of burnout, my body started to fall apart. I began to suffer from neurological symptoms as well as stomach pain and nausea. This only exacerbated the anxiety. There is something terrifying about being trapped in a body that isn't functioning right. You can't run away from your own body. You can't predict when it will decide to misbehave.

Sickness can pull the rug of security right out from under your feet.

The combination of anxiety, ill health, and a general sense of constant weariness brought me to my knees. Finally, I said, "God, I can't do this." It became a habitual inward thought. "I can't, God."

Life has a way of reducing us to our *I can't* places.

Just ask Esther.

Most of us are familiar with this famous verse when Esther's cousin Mordecai asks her to help the Jewish people: "And who knows but that you have come to your royal position for such a time as this?" (Est. 4:14 NIV). It's an encouragement we hold dear because it reminds us that God is in control of our times and places. That we have a role to play in His plans. That we aren't in this particular situation by happenstance. And all of that is true.

But when Mordecai originally speaks these words, he means them as a little slap on the back of Esther's hand. A tiny rebuke.

Mordecai has just revealed to Esther that their people, the Jews, are in mortal danger. He has asked Esther to intercede on their behalf with the king. To use her influence as queen in order to save a whole generation of their people from Haman's terrible plot.

And Esther's initial response to this heartfelt cry for help is essentially, *I can't*.

She reminds Mordecai that according to Persian law, if anyone appears before the king without being invited, they will be put to death. There *is* an exception clause. If the king himself intercedes on behalf of the intruder by raising his royal scepter of authority, they can be saved. But Esther doesn't have any guarantee that the king will intercede on her behalf. In fact, she seems convinced that he will not protect her.

You see, her husband, the king, has not sent for Esther in thirty days. And Esther interprets her situation through the lens of those thirty days.

She has been married for five years at this point. And for a reason the Bible does not disclose, her husband has shown no interest in spending time with her for a whole month.

A month of rejection.

Esther's response to Mordecai's request revolves on the spine of this heartache. This painful time of being unwanted. Unnoticed. Unloved. That's why Mordecai has to remind her of God's *such a time as this.*

God's timeline trumps ours. Our thirty days, or thirty months, or thirty years of rejection and heartache don't have the power to overcome God's *such a time as this.*

The last thirty days or weeks or months don't rule your life. They don't get to dictate your future. They don't have a right over you.

Often, when we have been reduced by life's hardships, we measure our ability by our human timeline and arrive at the conclusion that we can't.

Maybe that's where you are right now. Maybe all you hear reverberating in your mind is: I can't do this. I can't cope. I can't manage. I can't survive this. *I can't.*

But I want to remind you of the lesson of Esther: the last thirty days or weeks or months don't rule your life. They don't get to dictate your future. They don't have a right over you.

You belong to God's *such a time as this.*

Like Esther, I had to learn this lesson in my own life. I had to repent of my *I can't.* I had to capture that thought over and over again, and make it obedient to Christ. I had to agree with God's Word that He who had called me is faithful; He would surely do it (1 Thess. 5:24).

I had to learn an important truth. It is a truth I practice to this day: Jesus, with You, I can. I can walk through this wilderness and emerge on the other side.

Once your soul learns that truth, the roar of discouragement is diminished to a mosquito's buzz.

This hard season, this time of *I can't,* may turn out to be some of the most fruitful in your own life. So grab hold of God's *such a time as this.*

Be mindful of the places you are whispering *I can't* with God. Don't let them block your rest.

~~~~~~~~~~~~~~~~~~~~~~~~~~~~~~~~~~~~

LINGER

Have I been living according to the rejections and failures of the past thirty days, thirty weeks, or thirty years of my life?

Have I lost sight of God's *such a time as this* for me?

PRAYER

Forgive me, Jesus, if I have listened to the voice of fear or weariness or despair over Your voice. Forgive me if I am leaning into my *I can't* more than I am leaning into You. Please help me conform my mind to the mind of Christ. Help me hear with clarity what Your will is for this season. Jesus, I choose to trust Your *such a time as this.*

OASIS

Jesus, will you strengthen and help me? ~ Isaiah 41:10

Jesus, show me how I can give up my *I can't* and lean into Your *such a time as this.*

REST

But Jesus looked at them and said, "With man this is impossible, but with God all things are possible."

MATTHEW 19:26

Jesus, I rest in the fact that all things are possible with You. I know in my own flesh that I can't do this. But I receive the peace of knowing that with You I can get through this.

Peace Like a River

For thus says the LORD:
"Behold, I will extend peace to her like a river."

ISAIAH 66:12

Peace came for me and it will come for you too. The most astounding part of my experience was that I found peace before I found healing. Before I had answers. While I was still struggling with physical pain. Jesus gave me His peace before I understood what the solutions were. Before I knew what the future held.

Looking back, it's easier to take that peace for granted, because now I can see that, over the years, God has worked everything out for my good. But when I was in the midst of it, when the future remained inscrutable and scary, the peace I experienced made no earthly sense.

God can give you peace now, before you find your answers.

For me peace came in little bits at first, like shallow puddles that splashed in the midst of anxiety. Then the puddles grew larger and deeper, until eventually, God's peace extended to me like a river.

In fact, this is one of God's promises to broken Jerusalem: to extend peace to her like a river (Isa. 66:12). Although this is a prophetic word over Jerusalem, I think that we who belong to Jesus are also the recipients of this promise. We are part of the new Jerusalem (Rev. 21:2). God's promises of restoration to Jerusalem get deposited into our account too.

When God says, *I will extend*, He means that He will see to it that this happens. He will do what is necessary for peace to be extended to you.

Because God is extending this peace, He Himself is the source of it. *My peace*, Jesus calls it. "Peace I leave with you; my peace I give to you" (John 14:27). Not peace that is dependent on your circumstances or

healing or worldly security. That is perhaps the most beautiful quality of this peace. The wonder I myself have experienced again and again. Peace, when by nature I bend toward anxiety. Peace, when generationally on my mother's side I come from an anxious people. Peace, when my circumstances are overwhelming.

This is what Jesus wants for you. Plans for you. Extends to you.

If peace seems a far-off and improbable reality, remember Jesus' intention for you.

His peace has the qualities of a river. That means it flows continuously. It may have seasons when it narrows and seasons when it widens. But it holds within it a continuity of provision.

The waters that flow to you today are not the same as the day before. There is a fresh impartation of peace for each day. Peace that matches the particular challenges you will meet that day.

Like all rivers, you can dam up the waters. You can block them from flowing. I have done this myself when I have chosen to cling to fear, and not taken the effort to renew my attachment to Jesus. When I have poured my energy into things that have worn me out and not spent enough time in the presence of God.

Today, if you can, reposition yourself near to God. Renew your attachment to Jesus. Let Him deal with your catastrophic thoughts.

Ask Him to minister His peace like a river to your soul.

~~~~~~

LINGER

Am I blocking God's peace in some way?

PRAYER

Lord, forgive me for blocking the peace You intend for me to have.
Before I find healing, before I have answers, let Your peace extend
to me like an ever-flowing river. Let my mind, my heart, my body,
my soul, my spirit, my gifting, and my relationships all settle in
Your peace, Jesus.

OASIS

Jesus, do You really want to give me Your peace? ~ John 14:27

REST

"Peace I leave with you; my peace I give to you.
Not as the world gives do I give to you.
Let not your hearts be troubled, neither let them be afraid."
JOHN 14:27

Jesus, I rest in the peace You have given me. I quiet my heart in
Your peace.

Your Anchor Point

And they all ate and were satisfied. And they took up twelve baskets full of the broken pieces left over.

MATTHEW 14:20

My husband and I enjoy little adventures together. Last year, we took an archery class. When we arrived at our lesson, I was surprised to see stray arrows that had landed in all sorts of odd places. The walls, the rafters, the ceiling.

After a while, I began to empathize with the archers who had landed those wayward arrows. My left arm, which bore the weight of the bow, began to tremble with effort. The tips of my fingers burned from pulling the string.

Then I learned a lesson that helped me land my arrows even when I felt weak. Even when my body shook with the strain of holding up the bow. I learned about the anchor point.

The anchor point is a spot on the archer's face or body where he or she can rest the hand that is drawing the arrow. This simple resting place allows you to release your arrow accurately. It helps steady your aim even when your arm is tired and unsteady.

You establish a resting point for the hand that draws the nocked arrow, and repeatedly bring your fingers to the same spot: the temple; the cheekbone; the chin; the corner of the mouth; the neck.

Every archer has their own anchor point. It requires practice to determine what works best for you. What brings the most stability to your aim.

You can create anchor points in the spiritual realm, as well.

Places you return to again and again, which help steady your heart even in a season when you lack strength. When you feel overwhelmed.

There are specific promises that will have the power to calm your heart quickly and deeply. They act like a spiritual anchor point that helps you remain focused on God in spite of the distractions of your circumstances.

Jesus has a way of making sure that there is more of you by the end of the story than at the beginning.

Just like in archery, to create an anchor point, you need practice. You need to return to that promise again and again. You need to meditate on that particular revelation and study it until your heart can rest against it almost without effort.

I have learned to lean my weight into specific biblical anchor points. They help steady me when I am discouraged. They provide strength when I feel weary.

For the next several meditations, I will share some of my favorite Scripture anchor points with you. They may not work in the same way for you. But I hope as you read these passages that you will choose to create a few of your own biblical anchors.

Let's begin with the well-loved account of Jesus multiplying five loaves of bread and two fish until they satisfy the hunger of five thousand men in addition to the women and children in the crowd (Matt. 14:15–21).

For my anchor, I don't read this passage from the perspective of the men and women who sit on the hillside and receive the miraculous provision of God. Instead, I see this passage from the perspective of the bread and the fish, resting in Jesus' hands.

Like that simple offering, I am often vastly unequal to what is required of me. There just doesn't seem to be enough of me to go around! Not enough strength or wisdom or time.

Then I return to this anchor point story and I remember that I don't have to be enough. Jesus is an expert at stretching the insufficient to do exceedingly, abundantly more than we think or imagine.

What is lovely about this image is that by the time Jesus finishes, not only has the bread and fish not run out, but there are twelve baskets of leftovers! This world can make you feel like you are stretched so thin that there won't be anything left of you. Make you feel that by the end of this chapter in your story, you will be used up, dried up, with nothing remaining for you.

But Jesus has a way of making sure that there is more of you by the end of the story than there was at the beginning.

You may start as not-enough. But you end up being more-than.

Maybe today you feel like there isn't enough of you to go around. Maybe right now you feel like you are being consumed. But I want you to return to the bread and fish. Settle into this revelation of Jesus' intention for you.

By the time He is finished, there will be leftovers! More in you. More of you. More strength, more wisdom, more insight. More peace.

Spend time reading this story in Matthew 21. Spend time leaning into this miracle. Spend time picturing the bread being broken in Jesus' gentle hands.

Now meditate on the leftover baskets. Remember. That is going to be you.

~~~~~~~~~~~~~~~~~~~~~~~~~~~~~~~~~~~~

LINGER

Have I added to my anxiety by focusing on not being enough?

PRAYER

Lord, I am stretched so thin. I feel like I am not enough. Please multiply the fish and the loaves of my life. Be my anchor point, Jesus. I give You permission to break me and multiply me. I invite You to become the stability and peace of my life.

OASIS

Jesus, do You really love me? Bless me? Multiply me?

~ Deuteronomy 7:13a

REST

This hope is a strong and trustworthy anchor for our souls.

It leads us through the curtain into God's inner sanctuary.

HEBREWS 6:19 NLT

Jesus, I rest in You. You are, Yourself, the anchor of my soul. I anchor my life to You. You will not let me be swept away.

Your Wonderful Counselor

For to us a child is born,

To us a son is given;

And the government shall be upon his shoulder,

And his name shall be called

Wonderful Counselor, Mighty God,

Everlasting Father, Prince of Peace.

ISAIAH 9:6

One of the side effects of my anxiety was an odd reluctance to leave my house. This came as a shock. While I have always been a homebody, I had never experienced anxiety about being away from home. Now, visiting people caused a great deal of apprehension.

I remember one day a couple from church had invited me to dinner. They were lovely people whose company I treasured. But just thinking about going to their beautiful house made me cry.

I wiped my tears as I drove, realizing the monster of anxiety wanted to diminish my life and shrink it until I would be reduced to a tiny shadow in a corner.

I had to push back, or it would completely take over my life. I wept as I drove. Every cell in my body wanted me to turn the car around and go back home. But I refused to stop.

I had to fight.

At the same time, I discovered there were battles that I wasn't meant to engage in. Like the time my mother and sister and I had made plans for an all-girls trip to Florida. A couple of nights before we were supposed to leave, I realized what was meant to be a fun respite had become overwhelming to me. It was one thing to go to work or visit people. But I wasn't ready to get on a plane and stay in a hotel. When I prayed, I sensed that traveling wasn't a wise choice for me at that time.

I had to cancel my plans.

This was easier said than done. I couldn't face letting my mother down by not going. I couldn't bear the weight of her disappointment. Her unmet expectations.

This was one of those tricky situations where I could either protect her heart or mine. I couldn't do both.

That formed the root of the anxiety. My difficulty in proving to my own heart that I could protect it when it needed protection, even if it meant disappointing someone else.

In the end, what gave me the strength to make the right choice was the conviction I felt when I prayed. The right thing, the obedient thing, was to stay home. And thankfully, in spite of her disappointment, my mother gave me the grace I needed.

Two similar situations, and yet two completely different responses. One to go and one to stay. One to press in, and the other to retreat.

This is the discernment you will have to develop on your journey. When to fight back and push through, and when to take a step back to protect yourself. When to enlarge your world and when to make it smaller.

Take, for example, the Israelites who, upon arriving at Canaan, sent a dozen spies to scope out the territory. God had told them it was time to expand their lives. To settle in the Promised Land. The wilderness might be familiar. But it wasn't a forever home.

Instead, the spies returned shaken with fear. Swayed by their report, the twelve tribes refused to take on the battle (Num. 13–14). As a result, for forty years the people of God lived a diminished existence. A whole generation made small.

They lacked the discernment to realize that staying in God's will meant pushing back against fear. It meant fighting to expand their boundaries.

Don't make that mistake. Don't let anxiety and discouragement run away with your destiny.

On the other hand, when King Ahab of Israel and Jehoshaphat of Judah geared up to go to war against Syria, the prophet Micaiah warned them to stay home. This wasn't a battle they should fight. They refused to listen to God and charged in, and Ahab died in that battle. (You can read their full story in 1 Kings 22.)

One situation required the courage to push through, the other needed the wisdom to stay put.

You need discernment for this season. You need to know when to push back against the walls that are closing in on you, and when to listen to your heart's longing for protection and shield the wounded, vulnerable parts of your soul.

The good news is that you are not alone. Remember?

Jesus is your Wonderful Counselor through every step of this process (Isa. 9:6). What a mighty anchor point this name is! The word used here for Counselor is not a reference to a therapist. It refers to someone wise and insightful who counsels kings and leaders in difficult decisions. A sage and knowledgeable advisor such as found in 1 Chronicles 26:14. In other words, Jesus has the wisdom and insight to counsel you on this journey.

To advise you about the difficult choices you will face.

Today, ask Him for His counsel. Ask Him about the specific places where you should push back against the diminishment of your world, and places where you need to tenderly protect your heart.

I will tell you something. I travel all over the place now. I am still a homebody. But I am not bound to my home. One decision at a time, Jesus trained my heart for healing. He will do the same for you.

~~~~~~

LINGER

Have I been wise in my response to anxiety? Have I allowed it to make my world too small? Have I been a bad protector of my heart?

PRAYER

My Wonderful Counselor, will You give me the gift of discernment as I navigate this difficult season? Please counsel me when I need to push back against the boundaries the enemy wants to set over my life. Help me fight the diminishment of my world. Counsel me how to appropriately protect my heart in a timely fashion. Jesus, I give You permission to reign over every small and big decision. Have Your way, Lord, even when it is painful to my flesh.

OASIS

Are You really my Wonderful Counselor, Jesus? ~ Isaiah 9:6

Where do You want to lead me today?

REST

You gave a wide place for my
steps under me,
and my feet did not slip.
PSALM 18:36

Jesus, I rest in Your intention to give a wide place for my steps. I rest in Your ability to keep my foot from slipping. I rest in You, my Wonderful Counselor.

Your Breakthrough

He who opens the breach goes up before them;
they break through and pass the gate, going out by it.
Their king passes on before them, the LORD *at their head.*

MICAH 2:13

A few months ago, my husband and I took one of those once-in-a-life-time vacations on a beautiful beach in the Caribbean. It was winter, and being a resident of the cold hills of New England, my heart welled up at the first sight of those turquoise waters. I couldn't wait. I ran full tilt into the ocean.

I didn't realize that the seabed dipped quickly there. Before I knew it, the water came up to my chest. The wind was blowing hard that day. I saw a huge wave heading my way and stood helpless as it broke over me. Picked up by the sheer force of the swell, I tumbled roughly under the water and rolled a few times. By the time I emerged, I had sand everywhere.

I mean I actually had sand embedded in my nail polish! Even a couple of weeks later when we had returned home, the sand was still snugly caught in my nail polish. I had brought a piece of another country home with me in my big toe. That's how hard the wave had tumbled me.

When my husband and I stopped laughing, he explained that the way you navigate through this kind of wave is to not face it full-on. You don't set your eyes on the wave and let it roll over you.

You turn sideways.

That way, there is less body mass for the wave to come into contact with and, therefore, less force. When you stand sideways, the full expanse of your body isn't exposed to the wave's power.

To stand sideways, you have to take your eyes off the wave and focus on a different horizon.

The same principle serves us in our spiritual lives. Maybe right now you are being tumbled by wave after wave of discouragement. Maybe anxiety has embedded itself inside your mind and you can't thrust it out. If that's where you find yourself, I want to invite you to turn your focus from discouragement and set your gaze on an anchor point.

For today's anchor point, let's turn to Jesus, the One who opens the breach. In Micah 2:13, the Messiah is described as the One who goes before the captives to open a breach in the blocked places of their lives. He is the One who breaks through. In some translations of the verse, He is actually called the "breaker." The One who helps people break out of bondage and walk right into freedom.

Think of this powerful image: Jesus opening a way in the stuck places of your life. Jesus making a breach in that great wall obstructing your peace.

Can you trust the One who gives breakthrough? Can you set your eyes on the One who opens a breach in all the obstructions of your life and goes before you?

Take your eyes off the waves of fear and anxiety rushing toward you. Instead, let this be your focus: at this very moment, in the heavenly realm, Jesus is busy opening a breach in the layers of obstacles that stand between you and peace.

Turn away from the waves. Make the Breaker your anchor point.

LINGER

Jesus, where is my focus? Am I stuck looking at the waves, or am I setting my gaze on You?

PRAYER

Jesus, I have been tumbling in some overwhelming waves. Please help me. You are the One who opens the breach. You are the One who breaks through. You are the One who goes before me. Help me hold on to You, Father. Teach me to set my gaze on You. Teach me to stand strong, no longer overcome by the waves of discouragement.

OASIS

Jesus, do You desire to give me a breakthrough? ~ Micah 2:13

REST

And David said, "God has broken through."
1 CHRONICLES 14:11

God, I rest in this truth: You desire to give me a breakthrough.

Hold Fast

Show love to the LORD your God by walking in his ways and holding tightly to him.

DEUTERONOMY 11:22 NLT

A glass paperweight sits on my desk, the swirling waves of blue and white inside its clear dome reminding me of the sea. It's hard to believe that this beautiful object was once sand. It's harder still to believe that I made it with my own hands.

A few months ago, my husband and I attended a glassblowing workshop. What surprised me as I learned to handle the molten glass was how closely attached to it I had to remain through the process.

To be malleable, the glass had to remain molten, returned again and again to the blazing furnace, aptly named the Glory Hole. There could be no glory without that fiery hole.

I had to learn very quickly to manage the glass, which emerged from the furnace as a droopy thing at the end of a long metal rod, always in danger of flopping to the floor and shattering. The only thing that saved it from that ruinous fate was its close attachment to the rod, and therefore to me.

In this molten state, at its most fragile and weak, the glass could absorb color and be fashioned into a particular design. Sometimes I cradled my glass in a wooden block that kept it safe while being shaped; sometimes I subjected it to pincers and tweezers before inserting the unfinished paperweight into the Glory Hole again.

When I finished, I couldn't even take my red-hot paperweight home. It had to go into another furnace so that it would cool gradually or else it would shatter. A whole new oven to make it ready for the world.

Maybe you are like my paperweight.

Maybe, right now you feel unstable and weak, unable to hold yourself together. Maybe you have lost all strength and your heart is simply flopping around without an anchor for your emotions.

But I want you to know that the hands of the Maker are so close, they cradle you.

One thing I learned in my short stint as a glass maker was that every plunge into the fire had intention behind it.

The heat of the Glory Hole is never without purpose. I was not going to let that glass splatter to the floor. It had my whole attention. The glass stayed under my watchful protection, attached to me by that rod.

In the same way, the most powerful choice you can make as you navigate the Glory Hole of life is to remain attached to your heavenly Father.

In the Old Testament, God tells His people to hold tightly to Him. *Hold fast* (Deut. 11:22). He repeats this command several times to emphasize how important it is that we form a deep attachment to Him.

The Hebrew word used here is the same one used in Ruth 1:14 when Ruth clings to Naomi. It is the one used to denote the marriage relationship in Genesis 2:24, where a man leaves his father and mother and *holds fast* to his wife. It means to keep close, to cleave, to hold tight and not allow any separation between you and the object of your attachment.

Attachment is like the rod that kept me connected to the molten glass. It is the direct means of remaining under the constant rule and reign of Jesus.

One of the key ways of emerging from this season victorious is for your soul to learn this constancy of attachment to God because this depth of attachment opens the floodgates to consolation and guidance. Opens the pathway to strength and truth. Opens the way for obedience and healing.

You cannot hold yourself together. Jesus knows that. You only need to hold on to Him, and *He* will hold you together.

Some anchor points can work as relational attachment rods. Phrases or words that draw you close to God as they capture a specific element of your relationship with Him. You must spend time living out this relationship for the anchor point to be activated. Experiencing this particular intimacy in a personal way helps you lean into your anchor point quickly and effectively.

For example, just saying the word *Father* calms my heart and draws me close to God, because I have poured a lot of study and prayer into understanding what it means to be fathered by God. I have tasted the sweetness of that relationship.

Try creating your own "attachment rod," your specific relational anchor point that will help you experience an intimate attachment to God. Meditate upon and study a particular phrase that appeals to your heart.

If you had a fraught relationship with your earthly dad, *Father* may not be a good attachment word for you. Think of other words and phrases that describe God's relationship to you.

I like personalizing my attachment words to remind myself that a particular reality about God applies to me, such as: my Bridegroom, my Good Shepherd, my Deliverer (Matt. 9:15; John 10:11; 1 Thess. 1:10).

When you feel you are falling apart, return to your attachment anchor point. As you remember that you are not alone in the Glory Hole, your soul will be able to rest in the knowledge that rather than falling apart, you are falling into shape.

LINGER

Jesus, have I remained attached to You through this hard season?

PRAYER

Lord, take the soft, shapeless, weak parts of me and make them stable and strong. Form me into who You intend for me to become. Help me be malleable in Your hands. Jesus, I give You permission to teach my soul a deeper attachment to You.

OASIS

Jesus, do You intend to use this furnace of affliction for my good?
~ Isaiah 48:10

REST

Strengthen the weak hands,
And make firm the feeble knees.
Say to those who have an anxious heart,
"Be strong, fear not!"
ISAIAH 35:3–4

Jesus, I rest in You as You make my weak hands strong. Help me not have an anxious heart. I find my peace in knowing You will be my strength.

The Father Is with Me

"Yet I am not alone, for my Father is with me."

JOHN 16:32 NIV

There are a lot of reasons for feeling lonely. You can feel lonely because your husband walks away, your friend betrays you, your child rejects you. You can be lonely because you have lost the companion of your life, because nobody understands you, because you feel like you don't fit in anywhere, or because the pandemic diminished your community.

I find physical pain to be a lonely place.

I have struggled with long stretches of pain several times and always find it a solitary experience. No matter how loved you are, how accompanied, you are alone in the pain. No one on this earth can share what is going on in your body. You can talk about it with people who care for you, you can hold someone's hand, or ask for a glass of water when you take your pill. But ultimately, you must navigate the swells of pain alone.

Jesus experienced that kind of loneliness on the cross. He understands the brutal isolation of pain. But He also experienced the emotional loneliness of abandonment. After Jesus washed the feet of His dearest friends, He told them, "A time is coming and in fact has come when you will be scattered, each to your own home. You will leave me all alone" (John 16:32 NIV).

All alone.

Do you feel alone? Let me tell you something outrageous. Something that melts the heart. The Son of God, the One by whom all things are created (Col. 1:16), once felt all alone. When His prediction came to pass and His friends scattered, when His best friend denied ever knowing Him, Jesus felt all alone.

Into the soil of this sorrow, Jesus sinks the flagpole declaration that becomes our next anchor point. "Yet, I am not alone, for my Father is with me."

My Father is with me.

This promise offers an ocean depth of comfort. Because God is able to accompany you into places that other people cannot enter, or won't. All those nooks and crannies in your mind, all those places of unmet need, all those impossible twisted places of the heart that sit alone and unaccompanied. The Father can be with you there.

In His supreme moment of loneliness, Jesus found the Father's companionship enough to see Him through. His presence was enough to carry Him all the way to the end.

You may not be as aware of the Father's presence as Jesus was. You may not feel the consolation of His companionship to the depth that Jesus felt. This doesn't change the fact that He *is* with you.

My Father is with me means you can walk through the lonely places of this journey accompanied by His peace. Accompanied by His sufficiency and contentment and love. You can weep and know you are beloved when He gathers your tears in His bottle (Ps. 56:8).

In the Isaiah passage foreshadowing the birth of the Messiah, one of the names given to Jesus is *Everlasting Father* (Isa. 9:6). That means that Jesus Himself, as the second person of the Trinity, has a father relationship with us. That doesn't negate the Fatherhood of God. It simply means that Jesus also loves us with a father's heart.

If you are having a difficult time connecting to the Father, ask Jesus Himself to father you. To be with you in your loneliness the way a loving father would be with his hurting child. Ask the Holy Spirit to minister the presence of the Everlasting Father to your lonely places.

Know that the One who was Himself fathered in His loneliness longs to father you in your lonely places.

LINGER

God, am I coping with my loneliness in godly ways?

PRAYER

Jesus, my Lord, thank You that You knew loneliness for my sake. You have compassion for the lonely places of my soul as I navigate through this hardship. Dear Holy Spirit, please help my inmost being understand that I am not alone. My Father is with me. My Father is with me. Help my lonely heart experience His sweet companionship.

OASIS

Jesus, are You with me at this moment? ~ Matthew 28:20

Can You hold me and help me know I am not alone?

REST

"I am with you always, to the end of the age."

MATTHEW 28:20

Jesus, my Everlasting Father, I rest knowing that I am not alone. You are with me.

Small Thing

"This is an easy thing in the eyes of the LORD."

2 KINGS 3:18 NIV

At least once a year, I try to write a list of the ways God has blessed me in great and small matters throughout my life. One of the advantages of being middle-aged is that your soul learns the long view. When things are hard, you can look back over a long history of God's faithfulness in your life.

Everything—from my marriage, my work, my health, my friendships, my citizenship, to the birds that visit my feeder as I write this devotional— bears the hallmarks of God's power and grace.

I never grow tired of this practice. In fact, every time I do it, I become more aware of God's activity on my behalf. What seems an ordinary life at first glance starts to glow with the light of eternity. The seasons of suffering that might have led to bitterness, self-pity, and disappointment actually point to God's consistent work of redemption.

They lead to praise.

King David experienced a moment like this in his own life. After he was established as king over all Israel and returned the ark of the covenant to Jerusalem, we are told he "went in and sat before the LORD" (1 Chron. 17:16). In other words, he settled himself down for a proper heart-to-heart with God. And he remembered how far God had brought him.

His conclusion after this backward glance over his life is powerful. He says, "And this was a small thing in your eyes, O God" (v. 17).

Looking back over his rocky history—minding sheep, wielding a sling, playing the harp, living as a fugitive, running for his life, acting the madman, bearing the sword of a mercenary—David must have realized how unlikely a turn his life had taken. How did *that* man become a king? David, the great-grandson of a Moabite, sits on the throne of Israel!

By human standards this is impossible. Human will and human

intention cannot carve out this outcome. Cannot stitch that beginning into this ending.

But it is a small thing in the eyes of God.

These words act as such a powerful anchor point for me. What overcomes me, the situation that saps the last dregs of my hope, is a small thing in God's eyes.

In another impossible situation, the armies of Israel and Judah find no water on their circuitous march to war with Moab. They are in danger of being overcome before they even draw a sword. The prophet Elisha tells them that God will fill a dry streambed with pools of water, enough for the army and its livestock and animals. And the water shall flow without rain or wind. Elisha adds, "This is a light thing in the sight of the LORD" (2 Kings 3:18).

You may be in a desert place now. The way ahead may seem impossible to you. But remember this anchor point: This is a light thing. A small thing in the eyes of the Lord.

Jesus said, "With man this is impossible, but with God all things are possible" (Matt. 19:26).

Our souls tend to have a much clearer grasp of impossibility than of possibility. We can resonate with Jesus when He says, "This is impossible for you."

"It sure is, God!"

But we have more of a struggle internalizing Jesus' promise about God's possible. With God, all things. All things. Are. Possible. This struggle that overwhelms you is a light thing in the sight of the Lord.

Take a moment and write a list of all the ways God has blessed you. Remember the dark places He has redeemed. Recall that He is not finished yet. Bring your bundle of the *impossible* and rest in Jesus' *all things.*

LINGER

Jesus, have I been so stuck in my pain that I have forgotten Your blessings?

PRAYER

You are the God who overcomes the impossible. You are might and power. Majesty and miracle. You are my grace and my rescue. You are all the things I need. Father, I give You permission to change my heart. Pull me out of a despair mindset and help me taste Your hope again.

OASIS

Jesus, will You show me how committed You are to bringing me to the other side of this travail? ~ Philippians 1:6

REST

"This is a light thing in the sight of the LORD."
2 KINGS 3:18

Jesus, I rest in Your strength. I rest in Your power. I rest in Your majesty. I rest in Your overcoming victory. I rest in Your good plans for me.

Not Forsaken

And they shall be called The Holy People,
The Redeemed of the LORD;
and you shall be called Sought Out,
A City Not Forsaken.

ISAIAH 62:12

Earlier, I shared a bit of our sunflower saga. One of the beautiful varieties we especially looked forward to growing was supposed to produce dramatic red blooms. Every morning I started my day by looking at the sunflower plants. By now, they were about ten inches tall, and easily visible though they had yet to flower. One day, I looked outside the window. The red sunflower plant had disappeared!

When my husband and I ran out to investigate, we discovered that some animal had chewed the plant at the very base, not leaving any stalk. Further investigation unearthed the stalk, discarded under one of the bushes.

The animal that had severed it had decided it wasn't worth keeping. He had abandoned our treasured sunflower.

I wasn't about to make the same mistake. As the gardener, I knew the worth of this plant.

I brought that withered stalk with its shriveled leaves inside. It looked dead. Unwilling to give up, I cut the ragged edge and placed it in water.

The critter that had torn my sunflower apart might have walked away. I would not.

Remember this picture. Because at the root of many battles with anxiety you will find a wound of abandonment.

If at some point in your life you have been cut by the knife edge of abandonment, something in the marrow of your bones has learned its terrible lesson: it can happen again. You can be abandoned again. Unprotected. Unwanted. Cast off.

Left behind like my beautiful sunflower.

The wounds of abandonment enter into our lives by many doors. Through divorce or workaholism or even death in our families of origin. Through broken marriages and relationships in our own lives. Through words that demean and shred before an untimely parting.

Somewhere a whisper slithers its way deep into our bones: love cannot protect you from being abandoned.

For me, the lesson of abandonment meant that I had to work very hard to meet every expectation. A part of me had come to believe that the only security I could have must come from never disappointing anyone. Because as long as I was meeting expectations, then people would hold on to me.

They would not walk away.

To make sure I did not disappoint anyone, particularly those who were in authority over me, I worked beyond my ability. Worse. Internally, I never rested. Fear of failure chased me into every task. No success was ever enough to make me feel truly secure.

Somewhere deep within, I believed that if I failed, I would be abandoned again.

That is why I burned out. I was so busy trying not to disappoint anyone that I never walked in peace. My soul never rested.

Maybe that's where you are. Maybe an old wound of abandonment has driven you to a place of anxiety. Has stripped you of peace.

Perhaps, like me, you have tried to abandon-proof your life by carving your worth out of your accomplishments. Perhaps you are terrified that you might disappoint certain people, or fail to meet their expectations. Maybe you are on your way to burnout because you are unable to truly rest.

If you find yourself here today, let me tell you the rest of my sunflower story. In time, as I cared for that wounded stalk, my plant began to grow roots, at first delicate filaments that couldn't sustain in the soil. But those roots grew and thickened and became a wild ball, strong enough to survive in the garden.

You are Sought Out. Not Forsaken. God is rewriting your history.

When it was ready, we replanted the sunflower, this time protecting it with a special fence. The red sunflower overcame the wound of its abandonment. It grew tall and flowered gorgeous red blooms that lasted into October.

Do you think God cares less for you than I did for a mere sunflower plant that was here for one season and then thrown onto the compost heap?

Abandonment can become a block to receiving peace that passes understanding. It is a block that God always wants to remove.

Speaking to His people who had, by their bad choices and stubbornness, landed themselves in captivity, God says, "You shall be called Sought Out. A City Not Forsaken." By now, abandonment must have sunk into their marrow and become their identity, because God calls them by a new name.

Not Forsaken. Sought Out. The very opposite of abandoned.

Picture my husband and me beating through the bushes to find our sunflower. That's God, seeking after you. You are Sought Out. Not Forsaken. God is rewriting your history.

Invite Him to remove this block. Give Him permission to teach your heart to become Not Forsaken, even if that means opening your life to the possibility of failure.

LINGER

Do I have a wound of abandonment?

Do I try to earn my worth by my achievements?

PRAYER

Lord, I invite You to teach my soul a new name. Show me how to live as one who is Sought Out, not abandoned. Jesus, show me the moments, the situations, the words that allowed abandonment to claim me. Forgive me for believing its lies. Teach me to believe I am Not Forsaken no matter what others have thought of me.

OASIS

Jesus, how do I learn to trust that You will not abandon me?

~ Deuteronomy 31:6

How do I find that is enough?

REST

So be strong and courageous! Do not be afraid and do not panic before them.

For the LORD your God will personally go ahead of you.

He will neither fail you nor abandon you.

DEUTERONOMY 31:6 NLT

Jesus, I rest in the fact that You are not an abandoner. You will not forsake me. I find my peace and courage in knowing You will not fail me.

Your New Strength

We were under great pressure, far beyond our ability to
endure, so that we despaired of life itself.
Indeed, we felt we had received the sentence of death.
But this happened that we might not rely on ourselves
but on God, who raises the dead.

2 CORINTHIANS 1:8–9 NIV

Last year, when we visited my mom in England, she gave us a special carpet. It has been in our family for over sixty years. I remember it from the time I was a little girl, when it lay in the vestibule of our home. Every time a visitor came in, they stepped on it.

Looking at this little carpet, I am reminded of all the history it contains, all the memories it holds. It has traveled over three continents and survived three different climates. It has borne the dust of countless shoes. And our old rug still looks robust and beautiful.

There is a reason for this longevity.

My carpet is a Persian Bijar, which some call an "Iron Rug." These rugs are considered the most durable among Persian carpets because of the way they are made. They bear an extra wool weft within each row, which strengthens their foundation.

How is that additional weft added to the carpet? After a row of knots is completed in the pattern, an additional weft is *pounded* into the warp. The pounding, the beating, is what forces strength into Bijar carpets. It's what adds longevity to their beauty.

I reckon we occupy the world in order to become God's Bijars. Jesus called the devil "the ruler of this world" (John 14:30). That means that you and I live in enemy territory. Although Jesus' sacrifice has redeemed us from the rule of Satan, his influence in this world remains significant. Which is to say we will face seasons of pounding that seem unbearable.

Here is what I learned as I struggled with overwhelming anxiety: when you yield your heart to Jesus in the midst of your worst pounding, instead of destroying you, the hammer of your pain adds a powerful weft into your soul. The very hammer that Satan wielded against me came with a significant impartation from Jesus. The impartation of a deeper reliance on God.

During the journey, I was often only aware of the pain. Of the fears that were attached to that pain. But in time, I saw the weft of a new strength holding me up.

Over the decades, God's calling on my life has expanded. My responsibilities have multiplied. If you had placed these expectations on me twenty years ago, I would have shattered under their weight. The only reason that today I can bear the pressure of my calling with joy is that I walked through this valley years ago. That long process taught me not to rely on myself as much as I once did. Not that I have learned perfect God-reliance by any means! But there is more of Jesus in me.

He is, Himself, the strength at work in me.

Right now, perhaps you are in that hard place. You are feeling the hammer being wielded against you. Perhaps you feel a pressure that is beyond your ability to endure.

If that's where you find yourself, do not yield to discouragement. Yield to Jesus.

Part of the pain you are feeling may be the death of self-reliance. Even Paul, the faithful apostle, had to go through a season of despair in order to rise above self-reliance and sink deeper into God-dependence (2 Cor. 1:8–10).

Let Jesus remove the block of self-reliance from your soul. Allow Him to draw closer in your pain, and you will find at the end of this pounding is a new weft, undergirding your soul.

Jesus will use this pain for your welfare.

He will add the strength of His presence so that you can bear the weight of your future.

LINGER

Is there still a strong streak of self-reliance in me that Jesus wants to turn into God-dependence?

PRAYER

Jesus, my rock, my shepherd, my keeper, my lighthouse, my teacher, my wisdom, my hope, my love, my life, my truth, my way, my prince, my peace, my counselor, my comforter, my consolation, my strength: Jesus, I yield everything, everything to You. Teach me to learn God-reliance through this painful pounding.

OASIS

Jesus, help my heart grow more aware that even though Satan wants to use this circumstance for evil against me, You mean to use it for good. ~ Genesis 50:20

Jesus, show me You are truly trustworthy of my hope.
~ 2 Corinthians 1:10

REST

Behold it was for my welfare that I had great bitterness;

but in love you have delivered my life from the pit of destruction.

ISAIAH 38:17

God, I rest in Your promise that You will use this overwhelming season for my welfare.

Set Aside

My soul waits for the Lord
more than watchmen for the morning,
more than watchmen for the morning.

PSALM 130:6

When I had dated my husband long enough to know that he was the one, I asked him to travel with me to England so he could meet my family. While we spent most of our time with my folks, we did take one day to enjoy a tour around London by ourselves.

At one point, he asked if we could visit Hyde Park. By now the clock was creeping toward late afternoon, which meant we would have to leave soon to meet my sister and the kids for dinner. I told him that we could have a ten-minute stroll in the park. To my surprise, he turned me down.

It wasn't until we returned to the United States that I discovered what had really been going on that day. Knowing my sentimental connection to England, hubby had planned to pop the question while we were in Hyde Park.

Unbeknownst to me, that whole day, he had been lugging around a diamond ring in his pocket through London's famous sights, nervously thinking of the moment he would propose. By the time we arrived at Hyde Park, though, he realized he had to ditch his plan. He didn't want to rush through this moment.

Our schedule was packed with family commitments. This trip wasn't about the two of us. It was for the whole family. A time to get to know one another and bond together. He realized that if he proposed now, instead of being able to focus on building relationships, everyone would have to turn their attention to celebrating our engagement.

There is a huge distinction between giving up and setting aside.

Which meant that he had to give up his carefully laid plans. He had to delay his hopes, and lug that ring back to the US without putting it on my finger.

One of the things you may find as you battle anxiety, discouragement, or burnout is that you might have to set aside some dreams. Change some plans. Delay cherished expectations for a season.

When my husband realized that he should change his plan, he felt disappointed. He had spent days thinking about this moment. Now, it had been taken from him. But he also knew that he was not giving up on the dream. He was merely setting it aside.

There is a huge distinction between giving up and setting aside that the enemy does not want you to remember.

So many of the heroes of faith had to set aside their dreams without giving up. They had to wait without succumbing to hopelessness. Abraham had to wait for his promised son; Joseph had to wait for his vindication; David had to wait for his throne; Nehemiah had to wait for an answer to his prayer for rebuilding Jerusalem.

Setting your desires and dreams aside is a part of the faith journey. But holding on to the right things while surrendering the timing to God isn't easy. It's especially hard when you are in a dark place emotionally. Learning not to give up on the right dreams, the ones birthed by God rather than by pride or need, is difficult when you are sitting cheek by jowl with discouragement.

Setting a dream aside without giving up on it is an important decision you will have to make every day.

David understood this lesson better than most. He lived through so many discouraging seasons—hiding in caves, contending with danger, swallowing injustice, coping with betrayal and loss—that he had to constantly shore up his hope lest he be tempted to give up.

"I waited patiently for the LORD," he tells us in Psalm 40. I think that's the key to setting aside our hopes versus giving up on them.

David doesn't wait for the object of his desire. He waits for God.

Again and again, David tells us that He waits for the Lord and bids us to do the same (Pss. 25:3, 5; 27:14; 37:34; 39:7). If you find that discouragement is tempting you to give up, don't concede. If you have to set something aside for now, accept that delay. Give it into God's keeping. But don't give up.

Every day, remind yourself that even though you have to set aside a precious hope that was given to you by God, you will not give up on it.

Every day, commit to wait on the Lord.

~~~~~~

LINGER

Have I given up on something when God didn't want me to give up on it?

Can I choose to set something aside for now and wait on the Lord for its fulfillment?

PRAYER

Jesus, I give You permission to have Your timing in my life. Delay what needs delaying. Remove what needs removing. Restore what needs restoring. Holy Spirit, teach my soul how to set aside without giving up. Teach me to wait on the Lord without giving in to discouragement.

OASIS

Jesus, when I wait for You, will You incline Your ear to me and hear my cry? Help me hear Your voice as I read this verse. ~ Psalm 40:1

REST

Then Jesus told his disciples a parable to show them that they should always pray and not give up.

LUKE 18:1 NIV

Jesus, I rest in Your command that I not give up. I rest in You as I wait.

Aligned with the Spirit

When I married my husband, I knew there would be one challenge I would have to face from the first day. My husband is a morning person.

For him, 6:30 a.m. was on the late side, whereas for me, it was a form of torture. My body gravitated toward late nights and late starts. Two completely different schedules. Two different needs.

It would have been easy to keep our own schedules after we married. To kiss goodnight and part ways until the next day when we got home from work. But we were older when we married, and one thing that kind of long wait teaches you is to appreciate the treasure you have. I did not intend to miss a single moment of our time together. (This may not be a call on your life, by the way. It isn't a necessity for a happy marriage. It was just necessary for us.)

I started going to bed early with my husband. It proved harder than I had imagined. I would toss and turn, longing to get up and do something. I stayed put, because it meant being with him even though he was sleeping.

In the mornings, I would get out of bed, brush my teeth, walk him to the door, and kiss him goodbye. Then I would rush back to bed and grab an extra hour of sleep.

I think for the first year of our marriage neither one of us slept well. For me, it proved especially hard as my body fought the new routine. After about eighteen months, my new schedule started feeling more natural. I actually fell asleep when I went to bed early. And I started rising earlier and staying awake.

My body clock was retrained. Not by discipline. Not by work. But by love.

Love gave me the strength to lay down what I wanted to keep. It helped me to fully align my life with my husband's.

Love gives us the ability to do what we don't want to do naturally. It helps us overcome in the struggle between our flesh and our spirit.

In the garden of Gethsemane, Jesus sets the ultimate example for this principle. Jesus, who had known with absolute clarity what His mission on this earth was, asked the Father to let this cup pass from Him.

Why? Why did He ask for this reversal when every step and every miracle and every word over the three years of His ministry had been inexorably drawing Him to this moment?

Because Jesus was fully human. His emotions were like yours and mine. Susceptible to sorrow and grief and regret. His body was like yours and mine. Made of blood vessels and nerves and muscles and bones, vulnerable to hurt and ache and bruising. His mind was like yours and mine. Able to dream and choose and desire. And every part of His humanity, the part of Him that was attached to people and life and beauty, objected to the pain He had to endure. The untimely, violent death. The loss of every dream.

But He had to contend with worse.

His whole being recoiled from having to carry the putrid burden of our sins and experiencing utter separation from His Father for the first time in His eternal existence.

That separation must have been an unimaginable horror to Him.

His emotions cringed. His body cringed. His mind cringed. His humanity cringed. So Jesus asked the Father to take it away. All of it. This unendurable burden.

He prayed it a second time. Then a third. Mark tells us that He prayed, saying the same words (Mark 14:39). He prayed the same words, because the first time was not enough. His soul and body still waged a war with His call.

His spirit, though, was in perfect alignment with the Father. All the years of His life and ministry, His spirit had chosen to obey the Father in the small things, like where to sit and who to eat with and which direction to walk in. Like who to touch and what to say and where to pray and what time to wake up.

His spirit had learned obedience in the small things. And now that Jesus was facing the biggest thing, His spirit remained in perfect alignment with the Holy Spirit.

Jesus obeyed, as He always did because His spirit rose ascendant, and the rest of Him—His body, His mind, His heart, and His will—all fell in line. He was, even at this most awful moment, a human being operating out of the right order of His creation. His spirit obedient to God, and the rest of Him obedient to His spirit.

Because He loved. He loved His Father, and He loved you and me.

It was this internal harmony, this magnitude of obedience born of love that went to the cross. Not merely the suffering of His flesh, but the utter surrender of every part of Him won our victory. Our salvation. Our atonement. Our redemption.

Looking into Gethsemane, I realize that you and I will not be spared this battle any more than Jesus was. Half of our being will always want the path of less pain. Unless we let love win.

As you struggle in your Gethsemane, as you beg God to take away this cup, know that Jesus understands. He understands the battle you are waging. He understands your struggle.

He understands the prayers you pray again and again, because He prayed again and again.

When discouragement or burnout or anxiety sits at your door, let your love for God rule in you.

Don't underestimate the small acts of obedience that you choose to submit to even now. When obedience is born out of love rather than out of fear or resentment, it holds a power for your soul. That kind of obedience creates the building blocks of overcoming. Of peace.

Today, when the battle is fierce, choose another small act of obedience. And rest in His love.

LINGER

Jesus, is my spirit aligned with Yours?

Am I allowing my flesh to rule my life?

PRAYER

Dear Jesus, thank You for Your great love. For Your costly obedience. Thank You for living a life of right order even in Gethsemane. Lord, please help me be rightly aligned with You. Let my love for You increase. Help me pray again and again until I find a rested soul in my Gethsemane.

OASIS

Jesus, I don't know how to be obedient in the midst of this pain. But You do. ~ Hebrews 5:8

Will You please help me learn?

REST

By this we know love, that he laid down his life for us, and we ought to lay down our lives for the brothers.

1 JOHN 3:16

Jesus, I rest in Your love today.

The Lord Is My Peace

> *Then Gideon built an altar there to the* LORD
> *and called it, The* LORD *Is Peace.*
>
> JUDGES 6:24

A few years ago, my sister and brother-in-law rented an old villa in the remote hills of Tuscany and took me on holiday with them. We were surrounded by beauty: purple clumps of lavender; olive groves; narrow lanes bordered by tall cypress. But all that loveliness did not keep out an unwelcome guest. The third night I was there, I found a black scorpion on the stone ledge in the bathroom, looking like he owned the place. I knew right away that there was room for only one of us in that villa.

First, I needed a weapon. The handiest thing was my new shoe. The platform heel wedged the scorpion against the window. Believe me when I tell you the experience wasn't pleasant for either of us. The scorpion's hard shell simply would not give in. Repeatedly, it stung my shoe as I tried to squish it. The sting mark remained visible on the shoe for weeks.

Finally, the hard shell gave way and the scorpion died. Or so I assumed when it fell into the crevice between the window and the wall.

When my brother-in-law examined it a few minutes later, however, he told me it was still moving. Using a knife, he got into the narrow space and pierced the creature's hard shell. Now it was truly dead.

He dropped the carcass to the floor. Whereupon that scorpion started scuttling away!

I love the grace God shows Gideon in his battle with fear. He isn't vexed. He doesn't tell Gideon to pull himself up by his bootstraps.

It was like the Terminator. It just would not die. Eventually, a few more whacks from my brother-in-law truly vanquished it.

Some enemies are like that scorpion. They don't die easy. They return again and again to haunt you.

Fear is like that. It's hard to kill.

Take Gideon, for example. Before becoming a judge, he had already gone a few rounds with fear. And lost. He was hiding in a winepress, beating out a little wheat, afraid of the Midianites when the angel of the Lord first came to him. Gideon had been diminished heart and soul by fear, so that he told the angel, "I am the least" (Judg. 6:15).

When Gideon finally believed the angel, he built an altar to the Lord, and called it *The Lord Is Peace*. In the midst of fear, in the midst of overwhelming circumstances, God is peace.

But there is an irony to that title. The Lord Is Peace. Yet Gideon was still afraid.

When he tore down the altar of Baal because God commanded him to do so, he went at night "because he was too afraid of his family and the men of the town to do it by day" (v. 27). Later, when God led him to war,

He had to give Gideon extra reassurance because he was still afraid (Judg. 7:10–11).

I love the grace God shows Gideon in his battle with fear. The Lord isn't impatient. He isn't vexed. He isn't critical. He doesn't tell Gideon to pull himself up by his bootstraps. He doesn't shame Gideon because he continues to struggle with fear. God tenderly offers Gideon encouragement.

In the midst of repeated bouts of fear, God strengthens His child.

Just in case you have been impatient and critical with yourself because of your ongoing struggle with fear, please stop!

The LORD Is Peace doesn't mean you won't have fear. It means you persevere because God becomes the warrior you lean on. As my brother-in-law did, He sweeps in to help. Patiently, He gives you fresh assurances in the midst of fear.

I have found that the Father is incredibly gracious when I keep whacking at the hard shell of fear uselessly and watch it raise up its stinger again. Sometimes, Jesus takes over the fight. Sometimes, He strengthens my arms for battle.

If you have been going a few rounds with fear and are feeling weary, remember The LORD Is Peace. He is with you. He fights for you.

And show yourself a little grace!

LINGER

Have I become critical and impatient with myself because I can't overcome my fears?

PRAYER

Dear Lord, You are my Peace. Help me as I battle fear. Help me not give up when the spirit of fear tries to wear me down and wear me out. Remind me that I am not a slave to fear. When I am afraid, empower me to rest in Your grace.

OASIS

Jesus, teach me about Your peace. Show me how it is different from what the world offers. ~ John 14:27

REST

Peace I leave with you; my peace I give you. Not as the world gives do I give to you. Let not your hearts be troubled, neither let them be afraid.
JOHN 14:27

Jesus, I rest in Your peace. I rest my troubled heart in Your peace that passes understanding.

A Soft Heart

Submit yourselves therefore to God.

Resist the devil, and he will flee from you.

JAMES 4:7

One birthday, my husband surprised me with a basket-weaving kit. I had always wanted to try my hand at this craft. Most kits these days make life easy for the weaver, whether, like me, you are a beginner, or have a lot of experience. My kit included flat spokes, narrower "weaver" reeds, thin reeds for finishing, as well as a handle. I had to cut the spokes down to the right size for the pattern. After this, I had one more important step to complete before I could begin weaving.

I had to soak the stakes in water.

Although a kit includes prepared reeds for the weaver, you cannot use them yet. You cannot create a basket from them. In spite of their natural pliability, the reeds need to be softened further. Even the most malleable reed is still too inflexible for the weaving process.

Hence the soaking.

There is something counterintuitive about soaking anything woody, like reeds, in water. At the same time, the only way you can weave a basket is if you soften your reed first. Hard reeds are useless for weaving.

The heart has a good deal in common with basket-weaving reeds.

As you contend with this challenging season, you have to decide if you want to navigate through this suffering with a soft heart or a hard heart.

As I went through my months of anxiety and physical pain, I realized that this was a decision I had to make every day.

Every day, I could blame God. Resent Him. Grow bitter toward Him

for allowing me to suffer for so long. Separate myself from Him. Or I could offer Him a soft heart. A heart that remained yielded and pliable in His hands. A heart of submission.

Every day I had to make this choice anew as I soaked in the waters of pain.

Would I allow this soaking to soften me toward God? Or would I turn hard and resist the shaping of His hand?

A soft heart requires enormous humility and trust. Perhaps that's why some very famous people struggled with resentment for a season, Job, Naomi, and Jonah among them. But there is no going forward while your heart is hardened against God.

The only way to allow God to shape your life is to learn submission in the midst of pain. Like the reed in a basket-weaving kit, you may be just the right fit. Already pliable. But to fulfill God's plan, you still need a further softening. A deeper yielding.

Unlike the reed, you have a choice. You can refuse. You can go into that water and come out brittle and hard.

Or you can emerge malleable in Jesus' hands, knowing this is the only place your soul will find rest.

The heart can only be softened by repeated yielding, day after day, hour after hour. Every decision to be pliable in God's hand is like a single weave in the basket of your life. It counts. But it isn't the end.

Today, choose to have a soft heart in the midst of your pain. Resist the voice of resentment and bitterness. Resist the temptation to harden your heart. Today, submit yourself to God, even if you are soaking in pain.

~~~~~~

LINGER

God, have I been harboring a hard heart toward You? Or is my heart soft and yielded in Your hand?

PRAYER

Father, make my heart soft. Help me yield my dreams and my fears to You. Help me be pliable in Your grasp. I give You permission to save me from growing hard-hearted. I choose to have a soft heart today.

OASIS

Jesus, do You want to remove this heart of stone from me?
~ Ezekiel 11:19

Show me how not to resist Your intention in this.

REST

"Father, if you are willing, remove this cup from me. Nevertheless, not my will, but yours, be done."
LUKE 22:42

Jesus, I rest in Your desire to keep me from being hard-hearted. Not my will, but Yours be done.

You Can Withstand the Attack

"I will come upon him while he is weary and discouraged and throw him into a panic."

2 SAMUEL 17:2

Weariness, discouragement, panic. I have come to see a pattern emerge in my life that reveals a powerful connection between these three emotions. The Bible gives us a perfect example of the way the enemy can use weariness and discouragement, followed ultimately by panic, to overcome us.

When Absalom rose up against his father, David, he asked for the counsel of a very sly advisor named Ahithophel. Ahithophel, cunning to the core, suggested, "I will come upon [David] while he is weary and discouraged and throw him into a panic" (2 Sam. 17:2).

By now, David is worn down by his painful circumstances: the betrayal of a beloved son culminating in the profound rejection of many friends, the loss of his throne, and the physical exhaustion of being on the run once again. Ahithophel wants to press into that weakness to create intense trepidation in David's heart. To build up the kind of alarm that crosses his mental wires. He wants to throw David into a panic. Ahithophel knows that panic can reduce David to surrendering before he has even begun the battle.

Does this emotional pattern seem familiar to you? Weariness, discouragement, and panic? If so, it's because the enemy of your soul loves to use this particular formation of attacks against you just as Ahithophel used it against David.

When you are emotionally or physically exhausted, you are especially prone to discouragement. If you are experiencing a prolonged period of weariness, you have to grow more watchful over your soul, because discouragement might be waiting just around the corner.

You don't need to be suffering from panic attacks, which are episodic and physical in nature, in order to be battling a panicked state. They are just the cherry on top. If the cycle of weariness, discouragement, and panic is one with which you are familiar, know that you are probably under spiritual attack. Your enemy is trying to overwhelm and overcome you.

Remember that Jesus is still in charge of your life, and that life is precious to Him.

But he does not get to have the last word over you. With God's help, you can create a godly strategy to overcome this onslaught.

First, when you are especially weary, assume the enemy is headed in your direction. Ahithophel said, "I will arise and pursue David tonight" (2 Sam. 17:1). Arise and pursue! The enemy has an intention and a plan against you. He actively pursues you for destruction. And he is opportunistic. When he sees a vulnerability, he moves without delay.

Weariness is a door that often opens to discouragement. And when discouragement lingers, panic is not far behind. Do not allow your enemy to throw you into panic.

Remember that Jesus is still in charge of your life. Know that in the midst of this present suffering, He holds your life in the palm of His hand, and that life is precious to Him. Jesus will not waste it. He will not squander it.

Jesus still has many blessings for you. Small treasures to delight your heart and to bring God glory. Your work is not finished. Your life is not finished.

Stand firm on the foundation of Christ and don't allow these present circumstances to shake you. To have you. Don't invest your soul in fear. Don't give in to the temptation for despair. Despair is a lying spirit. Its very habitation is lies. Do not believe a single untruth whispering in your ear today.

Believe Jesus.

Jesus will not desert you. He who rose from the dead shall help you rise up from this grave of discouragement.

If you are weary, start seeking His protection and wisdom every day. Ask for God's strength to help you fight. To withstand the attack.

One final part of this story to remember: David could not face the battle alone. Which was why God sent friends with provisions and help (2 Sam. 17:27–29). There was an oasis of rest before the assault came.

This is an important aspect of your defense strategy, one I had to discover for myself.

Like David, I realized that I could not walk this path by myself. This was no time to protect my privacy. To pretend I had it together. I needed the encouragement and prayer of friends. I needed the companionship of those who became my oasis of rest.

Do not try to navigate this season alone. Find a few trustworthy companions. Those who are prayerful and wise. Men and women who have learned how to nurture a hurting heart rather than crush it with untimely judgment. David's men went into battle after receiving slivers of provision when their need was great. Look for this kind of short oasis in your life.

The enemy wants you to give up, sometimes before the battle even begins. That's why he adds discouragement to weariness. But at the first sign of his attack, tuck yourself into God's arms. Recognize the slivers of provision He sends you. Use them wisely.

LINGER

Have I missed the slivers of provision God has sent me?

PRAYER

Father, protect me from the attacks of the enemy. Shield me from panic. Help me not give up. Lord, I adore You and serve You and give You what is left of my life. I choose to withhold less and less

from Jesus until there is nothing to withhold. Holy Spirit, help me
trust You more and more through this season of weariness and
discouragement.

OASIS

Jesus, do You have provision for me? Will it be enough?
~ 2 Samuel 17:27–29

REST

I pray that from his glorious, unlimited resources
he will empower you with inner strength through his Spirit.
EPHESIANS 3:16 NLT

Jesus, I rest in Paul's prayer that still reverberates throughout
the ages. I rest in the knowledge that from Your glorious unlimited
resources You will empower me with inner strength through
Your Spirit.

Your Fortress

> *The name of the LORD is a fortified tower;*
> *the righteous run to it and are safe.*
>
> PROVERBS 18:10 NIV

A few weeks ago, I received several frantic attempts by my credit card company to contact me. It turns out that my account was hacked. Someone used my card to order pizza and Mexican food, and to generally have a good time. Over two dozen charges had been racked up on my account in a matter of hours. Fortunately, my bank refused to honor any of these.

We shut down the compromised card and ordered a new one. After just two weeks and five purchases, the call came again. Yup—the new card had also been breached!

Sometimes, it feels like this world grows less safe by the minute. Our sense of security, of safety, gets more tattered around the edges. If you are feeling anxious already, it may be because your entire world, the inner workings of your mind as well as the external circumstances of life, are constantly buzzing a warning to your heart: *You are not safe!*

You cannot have a rested soul when you don't feel safe. This is a block that must be removed.

Our ways of creating an illusion of security—our favorite escapes, our attempts at control, our human hiding places—prove useless. The suspicion that we really are not safe from harm finds us in the nooks and crannies of our mind like jam on a toasted English muffin. The fear sinks in and won't let go. To experience the bone-deep safety we long for, we need divine help.

One of the ways God imparts an assurance of security to the soul is by using metaphors of Himself as a hiding place. Images that capture who He is: our only place of true security on this earth. The only place in which we will find bone-deep rest.

Your heart will not intuitively find its way to God's safety. You have to train your soul to go to God as your secure place.

Today, we are going to focus on several different images that will help you in this process. You can pray through these daily. Meditate on the promise inherent in each image. Let them build a pathway in your mind until running to God and finding a sense of safety in Him becomes a regular habit.

One of the images that God uses as a metaphor for Himself is that of a strong tower. "The name of the LORD is a fortified tower; the righteous run to it and are safe" (Prov. 18:10 NIV). Towers, or fortresses, were common sights in Old Testament times. A fortress was often the largest structure in a city and served as a place of safety against various threats. People ran inside when the enemy attacked.

A fortified tower would have been a very evocative image to those who originally heard this promise. Places of refuge still dotted their landscape when Solomon wrote this proverb. They would have understood the sheer power of this truth.

God's very essence and nature makes Him a place of refuge for the believer.

Jesus opened the way for us to enter into that fortified place. By His sacrifice on the cross, by His victory over death, Jesus gave us the right to inhabit the strong tower of God's presence.

He Himself became our safe place.

We can hide in Him. We can take our stand in Him and know refuge. He is a champion who is ever ready to keep us shielded in His safety.

When we run into a fortress, our personal strength and ability no

longer matter. It is the impregnable walls of the fortress that keep us safe. There, we need no longer exert any energy keeping ourselves secure. We can lay down our weapons. God Himself becomes our safety, and we can rest within the walls of that true refuge.

To ensure that our hearts can rest in God's presence, He gives us several other powerful images. David says to God, "You hem me in, behind and before" (Ps. 139:5). In other words, the Lord is our rear guard and our vanguard. He is round about us, the way the mountains surround Jerusalem (Ps. 125:2). The eternal God is our refuge, "and underneath are the everlasting arms" (Deut. 33:27).

Think about these images. God hemming you in, going before you and behind you, surrounding you. And when you feel like you are falling, underneath are the everlasting arms to catch you.

Sometimes, life's experiences make it hard for the soul to truly enter the refuge of God. To feel safe in Him. Sometimes, your past teaches you that you will always remain vulnerable to hurt. To harm. That makes it hard to find rest for your soul.

The only way I know of crawling out of that conviction is one choice at a time. One prayer of trust at a time. One decision to cling to Jesus over fear at a time.

You have to train and retrain your soul to see the Truth in Jesus. He is your strong tower. Your fortress. Even if the worst should come to pass on this earth, He is enough. He will see you through.

When the storms rise, you can rest secure in Him.

LINGER

Have I lost my sense of safety?

PRAYER

Father, thank You that You are my fortress. You are my refuge. You are my strong tower. You hem me in before and behind. You defend me. Thank You that You set Your hedge of protection round about me. Thank You that when I fall, underneath are the everlasting arms to catch me. Help me feel safe, Jesus. Help me feel safe in You.

OASIS

Jesus, are You really a fortified tower? ~ Proverb 18:10

Do You really intend to keep me safe?

REST

As the mountains surround Jerusalem,
so the LORD surrounds his people,
both now and forever.
PSALM 125:2 NLT

Jesus, I rest in Your promise that You surround me on every side. I rest in Your protection.

You Are Favored

The angel went to her and said,
"Greetings, you who are highly favored!
The Lord is with you."

LUKE 1:28 NIV

Years ago, when I was in my twenties, I visited the beautiful island of Puerto Rico. We were traveling economy, but our flight was overbooked. As we waited at the gate, one of the flight attendants quietly approached my companion and me and told us we'd been upgraded to first class. To this day, I have no idea why they chose us. We had not put our names on a waiting list.

I only know that I was chosen.

Let me tell you, there is a world of difference between flying first class and flying economy. Our knees weren't scrunched up and our feet could stretch all the way out. We received slippers, a silky eye mask, and hot scented towels. Then the food came and we were transported to an elegant restaurant while looking at fluffy clouds outside our window.

We were given all this comfort and luxury without doing anything to deserve it. We never paid for any of it. We were simply upgraded.

You could say we were favored. The *Merriam-Webster Dictionary* describes the word "favored" in part as *providing preferential treatment* or *endowed with special advantages or gifts.*[2]

When the angel Gabriel calls Mary "favored," this is the kind of picture that comes to mind. The picture of special treatment. In my humanity, when I read that verse, something in me expects first-class treatment. The annunciation should translate into a travel upgrade.

Instead, there is no room at the inn.

This high favor comes with trouble. At first, Mary's betrothed decides to break up with her. Imagine the hard life she faces in a culture that has no room for unmarried mothers. Imagine the days of anxiety as she waits for Joseph to decide her future. When that disaster is averted thanks to God's intercession, more trouble awaits. Instead of spending the final days of her pregnancy surrounded by the comforts of home, Mary finds herself traveling. She has not been upgraded for this journey. The opposite, in fact. She had to lay her newborn son in a manger.

Later, a king wants to kill her baby. The small family has to run away to a foreign country and live among strangers just to remain safe.

This favor is troublesome. It looks nothing like the favor of the world.

Mary's miracle child, born of Spirit and mystery, would one day hang on a cross and die a painful death in front of His mother's eyes. This favor

---

2. *Merriam-Webster*, s.v. "favored (*adj.*)," https://www.merriam-webster.com/dictionary/favored.

can be excruciating. It is not the favor we imagine on this earth.

Of course, Mary also experiences the indescribable sweetness of carrying Jesus in her womb. The sheer overwhelming joy of it. The wonder and awe of it. She has the delight of raising Him. Every smile, every wise word, every loving hug a blessing beyond measure.

But let's not underestimate the trouble. The piercing pain.

God's favor sometimes looks radically different from our dreams.

Sometimes trouble and favor arrive at your door holding hands. Sometimes hardship is just the train of God's favor when it comes walking through your door.

I want to encourage you to look under that heap of pain in your life, and you just might find God's sweetest favor. Because when you belong to Jesus, you are already favored. Beyond measure.

The favor of eternity rests on you. The favor of the torn curtain. The favor of Jesus' intercession. The favor of His love.

The favor of being chosen by the One who is worthy.

Maybe, because life is hard right now, because your soul is weighed down, you have swallowed a lie. You feel anything but favored. Maybe you feel favor-less. If that's where you are, I want to invite you to reject that thought. Stomp on that belief.

The lie of being unfavored leads to disappointment and discouragement. It leads to comparison and jealousy. It leads to shame.

Your job today is to pull that thought out by the root.

Live the truth: in Christ, you are highly favored.

LINGER

Father, am I living as if I have no favor?

PRAYER

Forgive me, Lord, for living as if I don't have Your favor. Wash away this lie from my inmost being. Help me see that in my Savior, Jesus, I am already highly favored, honored and precious in Your sight (Isa. 43:4).

OASIS

My dear Jesus, are You, even now, covering me with Your favor as with a shield? ~ Psalm 5:12

REST

"The Spirit of the Lord is upon me,
because he has anointed me
to proclaim good news to the poor.
He has sent me to proclaim liberty to the captives
and recovering of sight to the blind,
to set at liberty those who are oppressed,
to proclaim the year of the Lord's favor."
LUKE 4:18-19

Jesus, I rest in the knowledge that You have brought to me the year of the Lord's favor. You have proclaimed liberty to me in my captivity. I find my peace in Your favor.

Little by Little

> "The LORD your God will drive those nations out
> ahead of you little by little. You will not clear them away
> all at once, otherwise the wild animals would multiply
> too quickly for you."
>
> DEUTERONOMY 7:22 NLT

Several years ago, my husband arrived home from work carrying four small tomato plants. One of his coworkers had shared her extra seedlings with us. We live on a postage stamp lot in suburbia. Our grass is treated with chemicals, so there is no way we can plant any edibles in the ground. Our only option was to try and grow these tomatoes in pots. We were amazed when, with a little care, our seedlings grew to produce more tasty fresh tomatoes than we knew what to do with.

The following year, we created a container garden using planters and pots on our deck. Over the seasons, we have grown cucumbers, tomatoes, zucchini, summer squash, green peppers, potatoes, peas, lettuce, beets, carrots, strawberries, and herbs.

We are mediocre gardeners. We still have seasons where nothing seems to do well. But whether we have a bumper crop or barely eke out a few veggies from our planters, we have learned one thing. The garden grows at its own pace.

Little by little.

You are not going to have a harvest overnight. Plants grow at their own pace. They produce according to their own timeline, not yours. There is no "all at once" in the dirt. You need patience when you are gardening.

Dealing with anxiety, burnout, or discouragement is like planting a garden. You may long for an all-at-once answer. You may be desperate to wake up whole. Without pain.

But this thing will have its own pace. Often, it only shifts in little-by-little increments.

When the people of Israel were ready to conquer the Promised Land, Moses told them, "The Lord your God will clear away these nations before you little by little. You may not make an end of them at once" (Deut. 7:22).

I imagine the people were disappointed by this announcement. Little by little? Why not sweep away these enemies at once? Why not get rid of the danger they represent right away?

Why allow the hardship to linger?

God actually has a reason for choosing the little-by-little method over the all-at-once. He does not want the empty landscape to be filled with wild animals that threaten the safety of the people and destroy their livestock. Too quick a solution only creates a bigger problem.

God always has a reason for choosing the little-by-little pace (though

He may not always share that reason with you).

This little-by-little pace will probably clash with the desire of your heart.

When I was struggling with anxiety and chronic pain, my deepest desire was to get past the struggle. I longed for an all-at-once solution.

But God chose the slower path to healing for me because His purpose was not merely to cure me of this present difficulty. His purpose was to wait for the full harvest. This journey led to fruitfulness, and God did not want me to miss out on the fruit.

Fruit is never produced all at once. It requires a little-by-little timeline.

If you are in a little-by-little season, don't resent the slowness of your progress. Don't despise the small beginnings of God's restoration work in your soul. Open your heart to Jesus' timeline. Trust in His objective.

Know that an all-at-once answer would probably open the door to greater problems that, like wild animals, would devour something good that Jesus has set aside for you. Know that when you give the government of your life to Jesus, there will be fruit at the end of this journey. I don't know the nature of it. But I know you can trust God to give you a harvest as you wait on His timing.

LINGER

Am I stubbornly clinging to my all-at-once desire even though that may not be God's will? Am I angry with God for giving me a little-by-little answer instead?

PRAYER

Father God, I long for an all-at-once answer. I long for an end to
my suffering. But Jesus, if this delay is of You, I will accept it. Let
me be aligned to Your timing. Holy Spirit, prosper this waiting time
with spiritual fruit in my life.

OASIS

Jesus, do You have a reason for this slow process?

~ Deuteronomy 7:22

REST

"Do not despise these small beginnings,

for the LORD rejoices to see the work begin,

to see the plumb line in Zerubbabel's hand."

ZECHARIAH 4:10 NLT

Father, I rest in Your small beginnings. I rest knowing that You
rejoice in the start of this work in my life.

An Honest Scale

Unequal weights are an abomination to the LORD,
and false scales are not good.

PROVERBS 20:23

God hates false measures. He warns us sternly against the use of inaccurate scales. For years, I thought of these scriptural warnings in the context of business. In terms of honesty in trade.

But there are other false measures that are just as harmful. Measures I have used in my own life.

When I was struggling with burnout, I slowly realized that my measures for success were skewed. My scales for an acceptable performance at work or in my relationships were not accurate.

Without realizing it, I applied a very exacting measure to my life. My scale required that I be at my best in order to be acceptable. My "best" left no room for error, for weariness, for busyness. I counted anything less than the best as failure.

And failure to me meant shame.

Those false measures pressed me into the arms of burnout because I didn't know when to trust God to cover my gaps. When to rest in Him instead of in my own performance or gifting. I had to be at my best at all costs so that I would not be ashamed.

Your starting point, your foundation, is that in Christ, you are God's beloved.

God does not like us to use false scales because someone always gets hurt in the process. I was using a false measure against myself and not even realizing it. And I was the one getting hurt.

David tells God, "But who can discern their own errors? Forgive my hidden faults" (Ps. 19:12 NIV). My false measures were a hidden fault in me, and I had not discerned them until I found myself lying in bed, staring at the ceiling, unable to function.

Sometimes, burnout is a simple matter of having no control over the hours in your day. A result of external circumstances you cannot master. Often, though, burnout makes itself an unwelcome guest in your house because, unknowingly, you invited it to come in.

When your measures of success are out of whack, you are flirting with burnout. If you always expect the best of yourself as a parent, as a friend, as a spouse, as an employee or a boss, your scales are dangerously broken. In fact, if you consistently ask the best of yourself in just one of these areas without leaving room for grace, start making a guestroom in your soul for burnout. Eventually, it is moving in.

Perhaps it already has.

Ask yourself why you have this false measure. Why you have allowed this hidden fault into your life, nurtured it, paid its dues, and given it power over you.

In an earlier entry, I mentioned that the root of my burnout could be found in an early wound of abandonment. I was trying to earn my worth with my perfect performance. I was trying to guarantee that nobody would leave again by making sure that I met every expectation.

That meant that my scale for being acceptable was completely out of whack.

How about you? Are your measures for success accurate? Are you able to have a rested heart even if you look in the mirror and feel the face and figure reflected there is just mediocre? Or if you come home from school clutching an average report card? Are you able to have a rested heart if you blow it as a mama, or mess up at work?

Are your scales for success, for being acceptable, accurate? Or do they land you in shame?

A life of right order starts with knowing that your worth flows from who you are in Christ. Not from what you accomplish. Not because of what you look like. Not based on what others admire about you.

Your starting point, your foundation, is that in Christ, you are God's beloved. You are the sheep of His pasture.

Are you able to inhabit that truth? Live it out? Be content in it? Wake up in the morning and, before achieving a single thing, know yourself utterly loved and, therefore, lovely, because of the crucified Jesus? What is getting in the way of you living out the fullness of your identity?

If you are beginning to discern a hidden fault underneath the ground of your burnout, ask Jesus to show you the root of it. Look for places of ancient criticism, or vacuums of praise. Look for areas where you were elevated solely for your accomplishments, not for who you were. Look for rejections and abandonment.

Bring all of it to Jesus. And let Him give you a new scale.

~~~~~~

LINGER

Have I been applying a false measure to myself?

PRAYER

Father, show me if I have been using a false scale for my life. Break me free of its power and pardon my hidden faults. I give You permission to reveal the root of it. I humbly ask You to heal me of old wounds, of vacuums of love and praise, of the scars of criticism. Please restore me. Teach me my true worth in Jesus, my Savior.

OASIS

Jesus, do You really love me just as the Father loves You?
~ John 15:9

Will You help me exchange my false measure for Your love?

REST

But who can discern their own errors?
Forgive my hidden faults.

PSALM 19:12 NIV

Jesus, I rest in the sure knowledge that all my hidden faults are forgiven in You. I rest knowing that although I live imperfectly and fall short, I am Your beloved.

Take Back That Throne

We destroy arguments and every lofty opinion raised against the knowledge of God, and take every thought captive to obey Christ.

2 CORINTHIANS 10:5

In my other life, I am a novelist. I spend a lot of time making up complicated stories in my head. That's a good gift to have when you write fiction for a living. But when you apply it to real life, it can get you into trouble.

You don't have to be a writer to fall victim to your imagination; all of us have the ability to make up stories about our situation. About our future. When you are worried or discouraged, those stories tend to bend toward the horror genre. Stories that claim your situation is hopeless. Stories that convince you the thing you fear most is going to happen to you.

It's amazing how credible your imagination can be. How it can convince you that the worst outcome is the only outcome. Sometimes, listening to the catastrophic thoughts in my head, I can be utterly convinced of the truth of these ideas.

The better your imagination, the more detail you are going to give the negativity that is building up in your mind. That kind of negative conviction is not from God. God teaches us to focus on what is good and wholesome. Some of us are inherently prone to negative thinking. But even those of us who aren't fall prey to negative thoughts when contending with a long season of discouragement.

Speaking about folks who are devoting themselves to false doctrines, Paul warns Timothy, "These things only lead to meaningless speculations, which don't help people live a life of faith in God" (1 Tim. 1:4 NLT).

Obviously, this verse is concerned with doctrine. It is dealing with myths and genealogies. Your problem is probably not stemming from those issues.

But let's look at the principle behind the verse. Paul wants Timothy to understand that we are not to spend our time, our mental focus and energy, on any speculation that is not advancing God's work in our soul.

Why? Because whatever thought pattern is not helping us live a life of faith in God is not good for us. That kind of focus will damage our soul.

If you are leaning into speculations that open the door to fear, to despair, to paralysis while at the same time keeping God's activity to a minimum in your story, then you need to stop. You need to train your mind away from false speculations. These things will damage your soul.

You need to fire yourself from the role of the scriptwriter of your life.

As convincing as your dark thoughts may seem—about what others think of you, about what might happen to your finances, your job, your family, your health, about the state of the world—most of them are inaccurate unless God has told you otherwise.

What do you do when negative speculations harass you?

Paul tells the people of Corinth, "We destroy arguments and every lofty opinion raised against the knowledge of God, and take every thought captive to obey Christ" (2 Cor. 10:5).

This is a familiar verse to many of us. Let me point out two facts about it. First, the Greek verb for *destroy* is often used to mean taking someone off their throne, or deposing a mighty ruler.[3] You will find an example of

---

3. "2 Corinthians 10:5," Bible Hub, https://biblehub.com/interlinear/2_corinthians/10-5.htm.

this word used in Luke 1:52, where the Lord "brings down" the mighty from their thrones.

How does this apply to your thoughts? You may have enthroned some negative conviction in your mind. You may have elevated a defeatist thought to take the Master's place in your life. A place of rulership.

That false master must be dethroned. "Destroy" doesn't mean you will never hear from it again. It means it loses the position of power in your life. No one gets to have the throne of your mind except Jesus.

Second, the Greek word for *captive* is a battlefield reference. *Captive* means a prisoner of war (Luke 21:24). You have to go to war against these false stories and take them captive.

The way to peace is through war.

You have to capture the negative stories that are parading in your mind as truth, and you have to put them away from you. Whenever one of them presses in on you, instead of entertaining it, entertain a truth about God that helps you live a life of faith.

Replace the false story with the true story. Replace fear with faith.

Ask God to help you believe the way Peter did after seeing the resurrected Jesus. Believe the way Paul did after the scales fell from his eyes. Believe the way Stephen did when the skies opened and he saw the angels. Believe the way the shepherds did when they looked up and saw the host of heaven.

Ask Jesus to build up your faith. Now let that faith kick out your speculations.

Take back that throne.

LINGER

Have I enthroned false stories in my mind?

PRAYER

Father God, help me believe the way Peter did after seeing the resurrected Jesus. Believe the way Paul did after the scales fell from his eyes. Believe the way Stephen did when the skies opened and he saw the angels. Believe the way the shepherds did when they looked up and saw the host of heaven. Remove every false story I have believed from my mind. I give up every speculation that stands against You, Jesus. Take up the throne of my mind.

OASIS

Jesus, will You send Your peace to guard my heart and my mind from the negative thoughts that beset me? ~ Philippians 4:7

REST

Fix your thoughts on what is true, and honorable, and right, and pure, and lovely, and admirable. Think about things that are excellent and worthy of praise.

PHILIPPIANS 4:8 NLT

Jesus, I rest in what is true. I hold on to what is worthy of praise and let the rest go.

The Consolation of God's Glory

Then shall your light break forth like the dawn,
and your healing shall spring up speedily;
your righteousness shall go before you;
the glory of the Lord shall be your rear guard.

ISAIAH 58:8

When I first began suffering from burnout, for a few weeks I lost the ability to pray. I simply did not have the energy or focus.

I remember one spring morning taking a long walk by the river when my eyes fell on a glorious sugar maple tree. The sun's rays landed on the young leaves, transforming them into bright jewels—peridots, emeralds, jade. I came to a stop, transfixed.

"You made this!" I whispered.

On the heels of that simple declaration, a sense of comfort flowed into me. A profound peace filled my heart.

A powerful exchange had taken place between heaven and earth in that simple statement. I had given God glory. I had acknowledged His power, His beauty, His control over the world when I looked at that maple tree.

And the result of that offering was an impartation of peace from heaven.

What is glory, and how do we give it to God?

A glimpse of the stars reminds you that the God who named them knows the number of hairs on your head.

In the Bible, the term "glory" is imbued with a complexity of meanings that can include honor, reputation, majesty, splendor, beauty, or a physical manifestation of God.[4] To give God glory means to see these realities at work around you or within you.

Certain things can awaken your spirit to God's glory and therefore to God. That beautiful tree awakened my bruised spirit to God Himself, the author of its loveliness.

By saying "You made this!" when confronted with the sugar maple, my spirit was declaring that God had the power to give life; that He could call forth extraordinary beauty from something that until recent weeks had been barren; that from winter's death, He had wrought a new existence.

The sugar maple pointed to the very realities that my soul needed to remember.

I needed to remember that God's power was able to bring forth life when I felt like I was withering. He was willing to restore and renew what seemed dead in me.

One of the most powerful acts of worship is to give God glory. To

---

4. E. F. Harrison, "Glory," in *The International Standard Bible Encyclopedia*, ed. Geoffrey W. Bromiley (Grand Rapids: Eerdmans, 1982).

enter into His sublime presence by means of a simple door.

Yes, this world is disordered and chaotic and foolish and heartbreaking. Sometimes, it makes no sense. But then you look at something as simple as the sunflower's seeds, perfectly arranged in order and function, and you realize that behind this broken world, the same Architect still works His beautiful order.

Your life is surrounded by innumerable such doors. A baby's first smile; the plumage of a tiny goldfinch; the ruby-bright seeds of a pomegranate.

A glimpse of the stars reminds you that the God who named them knows the number of hairs on your head; the One who holds every atom

of this complex universe together could have climbed down from the cross but chose not to for your sake.

Maybe right now you are having a hard time praying long wordy prayers. I want to invite you to give God glory instead. Train your eyes to perceive Him at work. His power, His wonder, His brilliance. Invite the Holy Spirit to show you the glories of God. To reveal to you the underlying consolations in His glory.

Isaiah tells God's people, "The glory of the LORD shall be your rear guard" (Isa. 58:8). The most vulnerable part of our body is the back. Our eyes can see ahead fairly well, and our peripheral vision can forewarn us of danger to the side. But our backs are vulnerable to attack. We can't see behind us to defend ourselves. Isaiah is telling us that God's glory covers our most vulnerable places.

Right now, your soul may feel vulnerable. Exposed. Fragile. But that is exactly where the glory of God becomes a shield. A protection.

Find a sugar maple. A sunflower. A rainy day. A white cloud. And give God glory.

LINGER

Have I taken God's glory for granted? Have I overlooked the shield of God's glory?

PRAYER

Jesus, You are glorious! I am sorry that I so often miss that truth.
God, help me see my life through the light of Your glory. Help me
grasp that You are strong enough to hold me together. That You
are mighty enough to call forth life in the parts of my heart that
are withering. That You are loving enough to bring new life out of
this season of diminishment. I give You glory, Lord. You are able.

OASIS

Lord, what does it mean that You are the glory in my midst?

~ Zechariah 2:5

REST

*"And I will be to her a wall of fire all around, declares the LORD, and I
will be the glory in her midst."*

ZECHARIAH 2:5

Jesus, I rest knowing You are a wall of fire all around me, just as You
were for beleaguered Jerusalem.

Your Rescue

"And the patriarchs, jealous of Joseph, sold him into Egypt;
but God was with him and rescued him out of all his
afflictions and gave him favor and wisdom before Pharaoh,
king of Egypt, who made him ruler over Egypt and over
all his household."

ACTS 7:9–10

Sometimes God's rescues don't look like what you expected.

Years ago, I started suffering from persistent headaches. They were always on the same side of my head. Headaches are pesky things to live with, and this one proved particularly disagreeable. Tests showed that my sinus was completely blocked. After a course of strong antibiotics, further tests showed that the blockage had opened, but this time, the sinus on the opposite side of my face was completely blocked.

I felt discouraged, because fixing my sinus had not fixed my headache. "How odd," I told the specialist. "My head still hurts on the same side."

The specialist called me the next day and told me a strange thing.

After speaking to me, he had decided to call the radiologist. "Can you read that film again, please? Can you make sure you didn't flip the film?"

Yup. That is exactly what had happened. The blockage in my sinus had never opened. The same sinus remained blocked.

Now I needed surgery. A relatively simple procedure to remove polyps. I was delighted, because surgery would mean the headaches would stop.

Except surgery showed that beneath the fat, benign polyps sat a nasty little tumor that could become cancerous. I needed a second more complicated surgery to remove it because it was located in a tricky area. Only eight surgeons in our state even had the ability to do this procedure.

But as we prepared for the surgery, tests revealed that the tumor seemed smaller and in an easier location than the first surgeon had detected. I explained to my surgeon that we had been praying. I knew where the credit for this unexpected improvement lay.

The second surgery went smoothly. The tumor was removed successfully. It has stayed gone and the doctors don't even want to see me for annual checkups anymore.

That tumor could have led to an ugly disease. A long illness culminating in death. It never got the chance to do that. God rescued me. And He used a pesky headache to do it. The very thing I desperately wanted gone saved my health.

If that initial headache had not been so exhausting, I would never have gone to the doctor in the first place. If it had not persisted, he wouldn't have bothered to follow up with the radiologist to discover an unexpected mistake. Because he followed up, we realized that I needed surgery. It was only in the course of that surgery that they discovered the tumor growing like a ticking time bomb inside my sinus.

God used a painful headache to save me.

Sometimes, Jesus uses odd instruments for His rescues.

Take Joseph. His world started to unravel when his brothers decided to kill him. Reuben, the oldest, intervened to save Joseph's life by convincing the others to throw him into an empty cistern instead. He used a pit as a means of deliverance.

Sometimes, God allows you to be thrown into a pit to save your life. To give you a future.

But the pit wasn't a big enough rescue. Joseph's brothers were not the only danger that loomed over his life. God knew that a greater threat was coming not merely against this young man, but against the whole lineage of Abraham. So He sent a greater rescue. A caravan of Ishmaelites. The brothers sold him, and God's second rescue showed up as the yoke of slavery for Joseph.

I dare say that, not knowing about the looming famine in his future, Joseph did not consider that caravan as a rescue. But it was. It was the means of a grand salvation.

You may be in a caravan right now, heading for where you don't want to go. But God can use this to bring a future rescue.

Joseph found an oasis in Potiphar's household. Though a slave, he was elevated to a position of authority, enjoying a measure of comfort and security. His heart may have longed for his father and brothers and home. But his position provided him with ease. Joseph might have been content to stay there. To make the oasis his forever home.

But God was not. God allowed the next rescue to come through the dishonest lips of a vindictive woman. This time, Joseph's rescue came in the form of prison.

Joseph could not stand next to the throne unless he first sat in the jail.

He could not wield the kind of authority that delivered generations of his people from famine until he sank into another pit.

If you are moldering in confinement, your gifts hampered, your purpose obstructed, don't think God has forgotten about you. This could very well be part of His rescue plan.

Joseph's final rescue from his affliction came through a miracle. With God's help, Joseph interpreted his cellmates' dreams. Ultimately, this divine wisdom led to Joseph's freedom and the governorship of Egypt.

Have you noticed how as Joseph's afflictions expand, God's rescues grow more powerful? If you have been stuck in a long period of suffering, know that God's deliverance will match the size of your pain.

But sometimes it's hard to recognize God's rescues for what they are. He uses what is at hand in this fractured world to get us to where we need to go. Maybe, right now, in this broken season, God's rescue is buried in the ground of your affliction.

For Joseph, the grand rescue, the one we all recognize as deliverance, the moment Joseph saves the Hebrews from famine, does not come until the end of the story. It requires years to fulfill. Sometimes, God's grand rescues are only recognizable months and years down the road of your life. In the interim, there are the in-between rescues.

Strangely, the healing of Joseph's heart is almost the final piece in the puzzle of his broken life. He doesn't find emotional healing until all the other rescues are in place.

Your heart may be the last piece to heal. The final rescue. That doesn't mean God has overlooked your heart. He is just bringing all the rescues into place.

Perhaps you have been leaning into discouragement. Maybe, looking at the pits and prisons of your life, you have assumed God is late. Disinterested. Impotent.

If that's where you are, start training your eyes to recognize God's rescues. Look to the Scriptures to see evidence of His hand at work in life's valleys. Examine your own life. See if you can unearth a few unusual rescues of your own.

~~~~~~

LINGER

Have I missed some of God's rescues in my life because they didn't look like what I expected?

PRAYER

Lord Jesus, my deliverer, help me to rest knowing that You can use all the broken pieces around me for good. Increase my trust in You when I am in the pit. Rescue me, and keep on rescuing me, Lord, even as You did Joseph.

OASIS

Jesus, are You with me? Do You want to rescue me? ~ Acts 7:9–10

REST

And after you have suffered a little while, the God of all grace, who has called you to his eternal glory in Christ, will himself restore, confirm, strengthen, and establish you.
1 PETER 5:10

Jesus, I rest in Your promise that You will, Yourself, restore me. You will confirm, strengthen, and establish me.

Your Rest

Jesus said to them, "Come and have breakfast."

JOHN 21:12

Last week, I fell behind on my work. My to-do list was growing instead of diminishing no matter how hard I tried to whittle it down. I looked at the pile on my desk and made an important decision. It was time to have a picnic in the rose park.

Sometimes, it's really important to take a breath.

Jesus knows we are dust. He knows our bodies need rest. He knows our souls are affected by the rhythms of our bodies.

Even though those pesky troubles aren't resolved and the problems aren't taken away, sometimes Jesus wants you to have rest right alongside the things that shake you. He lets both of them stand at the same time.

He provides for simple moments of rest in the midst of our troubles. Just like He did for the disciples.

After the resurrection, seven of the disciples decided to go fishing. They got into their boat, plied their considerable skills and their strength all night, and came up empty-handed.

A little sidebar here. You know you can be tired even if you don't have anything to show for it, right? That you can be legitimately exhausted even when you haven't been productive? That you need rest not based on what you produce, but on how much energy you have expended, and how weary you are?

Jesus knows that.

At daybreak, when the disciples come ashore from their wasted night, Jesus is waiting for them. "Come and have breakfast," He says.

Can you imagine? The Messiah is risen from the dead! The church needs building. The world needs saving. The poor confused disciples need explanations. There is a lot of work that needs doing. But Jesus starts by making breakfast for His friends.

I am telling you this in case you have a hard time taking care of yourself.

Jesus knows there is so much that needs your attention. But He still wants to take care of your simple needs.

He supplies simple rest for the disciples in several ways. First, He fills their empty nets with 153 large fish. I have to stop and mention how awesome it is that someone counted every single fish, and then made sure it was recorded for posterity. You can tell it's a fisherman who is recounting this story.

So instead of having empty nets, Jesus fills the disciples' nets with 153 fish. Where the world leaves them empty-handed, He provides. God's provision is a form of rest because lack can exhaust you.

When He provides that extraordinary catch, Jesus ensures that the nets aren't torn. They hold together even though the burden they hold is great. If your burden is too heavy, rest in the One who does not allow the nets to tear.

And then comes my favorite moment. Jesus cooks breakfast for His friends so that they can be restored after their long night.

Sometimes, the ordinary things need care first. The empty net needs to fill. The hunger needs to be satisfied. We are creatures of the Spirit. Miracle-making, miracle-receiving eternal beings. But we are also simple biological things. Jesus never overlooks that.

You shouldn't either. Part of having a rested soul is to make sure you take time for simple rest.

Which is why I went to the rose park even though my pile of work glared at me balefully and demanded my attention. That day, I sat on a park bench across from a bush that had multicolored blooms all on the same plant. Some were pink and white; some were yellow and orange. It looked like something that shouldn't be possible. One bush producing completely different colored roses.

It dawned on me as I looked at that profusion of opposing shades that life is meant to be lived like that. Our souls were created to have rest even while juggling stress. Like different colored roses sprouting out of the same bush, we were created to have peace even when the weight of responsibility sometimes overwhelms us.

God has given us the capacity to experience the impartations of heaven: a rested soul; a quiet mind; a joyful heart, while also bearing the disquiet of this world. The impartations of heaven can fit right into whatever is going on in your life. Anxiety. Burnout. Discouragement.

Start with some simple moments of rest. The Jesus who invited His tired friends to come and have breakfast, to sit and rest after a long night, wants no less for you.

~~~~~~

LINGER

Have I believed that I am only worthy of receiving rest if I am productive?

Do I have a hard time taking care of myself the way Jesus would want?

PRAYER

Lord Jesus, thank You that You choose to fill my empty net. Thank You that when my burden grows too heavy, You will not allow me to be torn apart under its weight. Thank You that You care for the ordinary needs of my life and my body. Thank You that You know I am dust, and You make provision for my weakness.

OASIS

Jesus, do You really want me to have moments of ease? Of simple rest? ~ John 21:12

REST

For he knows our frame;
he remembers that we are dust.

PSALM 103:14

Father, I rest knowing that You understand my frailty even though I myself sometimes don't.

Contending
for Contentment

For I have learned in whatever situation I am to be content.
I know how to be brought low, and I know how to abound.
In any and every circumstance, I have learned the secret of
facing plenty and hunger, abundance and need.
PHILIPPIANS 4:11–12

When you wrestle with discouragement for a long time, sometimes another uninvited guest makes itself at home in your mind.

Disappointment.

You can be disappointed in two basic ways: with the shape of your life, or with God. You can feel disappointed because this was not the life you signed up for. Or you can be disappointed because God did not give you the healing or restoration or protection you wanted. Sometimes the two disappointments play ping-pong in your heart.

I don't think disappointment itself is a sin. It's a natural by-product of pain. A leftover of Eden's memories that make you realize this present experience is nothing like what your life was created to be.

But disappointment does make you vulnerable to sin.

I am reminded of what God told Cain. "Sin is crouching at your door; it desires to have you, but you must rule over it" (Gen. 4:7 NIV). Sometimes, sin scooches right over to your door. Like a preying tiger, it crouches inches away from you, ready to pounce. Disappointment slides you right over to that door where sin is crouching. It gives sin easy access to you.

When I sank into disappointment, I noticed that I became vulnerable to two particular sins: self-pity and discontentment. The sins that crouch at your door may be different. For me, these were the specific sins that desired to have me. The sins I had to rule over.

Self-pity is a nasty little beast. It makes you lose your hold on joy. It forces your eyes away from God and sets them on yourself. It carefully measures everything that's wrong. Everything that hurts. It cradles pain like it's a best friend.

Self-pity's cousin is discontentment. You have to watch out for this one, because sometimes it slithers into your veins through your generational lines. Before you ever enter the ring of battle, you learn to be discontented. To have your eyes on the thing you don't have.

Whether you learned discontentment in your family of origin, or it was a late addition to your soul, it will rob your joy.

Worse. Discontentment is a thief of gratitude.

Perhaps the most helpful weapon I had as I fought against these two sins was Paul's famous words: "For I have learned in whatever situation I am to be content" (Phil. 4:11).

The context of this verse is financial. Paul is talking about being content whether he has sufficiency or he is struggling in need. But when you read his other writings, you will find that Paul has learned contentment in every area of his life. The man who sang hymns to God after a brutal beating knows how to be content while in physical pain (Acts 16:23–25). The man who says "Rejoice in the Lord always; again I will say, rejoice" while languishing in prison knows how to be content when life has proven hard and disappointing (Phil. 4:4).

Paul knows contentment. But he wasn't born with it. He tells us that he has *learned* to be content.

This was the seed of hope for me as I faced my two crouching sins. I realized that I could *learn* to be content even though my life seemed to be falling apart. And if I could be content, there was no reason to engage in self-pity.

The first step to ruling over the sin that is crouching at your door while you are in the valley is to recognize it's there. To name it. To know its voice when it comes knocking at your door. What is it that desires to have you? Be quick in identifying it.

The greatest weapon I found against my particular sins was gratitude. I begin each day with a preemptive strike. I list at least three, often many more, specific things for which I am thankful. Even if you don't *feel* thankful, press into gratitude by spending time naming things that are good in your life. Train your mind to recognize these things. The feelings will eventually come.

Gratitude is an intention. You can choose to activate it throughout your day. When self-pity descends like a vulture, acknowledge the pain it is complaining about. Then lift up that pain to God. Thank Him for the gift of His presence. He is in this pain with you. He accompanies you. Focus more on Him than on the pain.

Over the years I have learned to be a lot more contented than I could have imagined. I find joy easily, even when life is hard. Not that I am perfect at it. But I have experienced a profound transformation.

For me, this internal change did not come overnight. It came over many hours of practicing gratitude.

One final thought if you are struggling to feel grateful right now. It is important to acknowledge your pain. I am not suggesting that you bury it. Indeed, it's important to look for the true root of your discouragement or anxiety. Seek healing for those wounded places. That requires reliving some past hurts. But don't confuse self-pity for the healing path. You can have compassion for the wounded parts of you. Jesus certainly does. You just don't need to jump into the well of pain with both feet and make your home in it.

Today, be mindful of the disappointment that is percolating in your soul. Choose to activate gratitude in your heart. Resist self-pity as you walk through healing.

Contend for your contentment.

~~~~~~

LINGER

Am I feeling disappointed with my life?
Am I feeling disappointed with God?

What are the sins crouching at my door, eager to control me?

Am I activating gratitude in my life?

PRAYER

Lord, I lift up my disappointment to You. This isn't how I thought my life would turn out. This isn't how I thought You would provide for me. Jesus, protect this vulnerable place in my soul. Don't let sin control me. Don't allow disappointment to rob me of gratitude and joy. I give You permission to transform me through this journey. Teach me to be content in every circumstance.

OASIS

Jesus, is Your desire that I learn contentment? Can You help me resist the sin that waits at the door of my disappointment?

REST

And God is able to make all grace abound to you, so that having all sufficiency in all things at all times, you may abound in every good work. 2 Corinthians 9:8

Jesus, I rest knowing that You are able to make all grace abound to me. Grace to teach me contentment. Grace to help me see Your all-sufficiency at work in my life.

Victory Over Discouragement and Pain

For you have need of endurance, so that when you have done
the will of God you may receive what is promised.

HEBREWS 10:36

Several times in my life, I have had to contend with periods of chronic physical pain. The kind that doesn't kill you, but wears you down.

Whether physical or psychological, pain, when it lingers, has a way of welcoming another uninvited guest. Discouragement.

The enemy uses discouragement like a veil that he draws over pain, because pain comes bearing a few gifts that the enemy doesn't want you to see. If you manage to pull the curtain of discouragement aside, you may just find a few wonders hiding behind that unpleasant façade.

One of the greatest treasures you will find in pain is the Father's love. In that dark well, God does not wait in indifference. He waits in love.

This is the place where the soul learns that God's love is *enduring*. Your love may fail. But His love never fails. Never ends. It endures all things

(1 Cor. 13:7–8). Pain does not have the power to erode the Father's love.

God's love is a key ingredient to bearing this season. To emerging from it victorious. The Father's love makes it possible for your soul to learn patient endurance.

If in the midst of suffering from sustained pain you manage to become aware that the Father is holding you, nurturing you, loving you, something in your soul is empowered to endure. For a minute. For ten minutes. For an hour. You learn to endure little by little, strengthened by the love of God.

Patient endurance is an odd thing. Like a bumblebee flying, it should technically be impossible. Because patient endurance arises out of the kind of suffering that wears you out. Wears you down. Makes you fragile. Makes you breakable.

At the same time, patient endurance gives rise to an odd sort of resilience. A kind of unbreakable quality. So you become both at once: your most breakable in the flesh and your most unbreakable in the spirit.

When you are walking through persistent pain, your soul is much more in touch with the breakable part. With the I-can't-endure-this-anymore part. But when you cling to God, when you cry, *Father*, and don't let go, when you give your hand for Jesus to hold, when His love starts to tear through that curtain of discouragement, then right along those feelings of breakability, something unbreakable builds up in your soul.

A wellspring of peace that is not easily shaken.

The doorway to patient endurance is the love of God. It's the treasure that waits for you behind discouragement.

If you have been walking through pain, emotional, psychological, or physical, look for God's love in the midst of it. Pluck out the lies that have landed in your heart. God is not indifferent. He is not cruel. He loves you with a sustained and tender passion that will not let go.

~~~~~~~~~~~~~~~~~~~~~~~~~~~~

LINGER

Have I been blinded to Your love in the midst of my discouragement?

PRAYER

Father, let Your unfailing love surround me. Let Your enduring love calm me. Let Your loving hand hold me. Tear the curtain of discouragement that separates me from Your love. Teach my soul patient endurance.

OASIS

Jesus, is Your love for me truly enduring, unending, unconditional?
~ 1 Corinthians 13:7–8

REST

Love bears all things, believes all things,
hopes all things, endures all things.
Love never ends.
1 CORINTHIANS 13:7–8

Jesus, I rest in Your love.

Life Is Beautiful

The LORD your God is in your midst,
a mighty one who will save;
he will rejoice over you with gladness;
he will quiet you by his love;
he will exult over you with loud singing.

ZEPHANIAH 3:17

My father used to tell me, "Don't forget that life is beautiful." He said that he couldn't remember a time in his life when he wasn't aware of this reality. Even when he lived through the revolution, diminished by his long season of depression and anxiety, he still knew that life was beautiful.

On this final day of our journey together, I want to remind you of this reality. Your life is a beautiful gift from God.

Affliction has a way of stealing that truth from your heart. Satan likes using pain to rob you of the joy of life. But God wants you to grasp hold of it. To see the beauty in the ordinary and the extraordinary.

As a follower of Jesus, your eyes never open to a morning that is not undergirded by God's help. Paul, writing from prison, declares, "To this day I have had the help that comes from God" (Acts 26:22).

Your feet never touch a ground not carpeted by God's grace. You are constantly accompanied by a kind God who covers your failures with grace.

Your heart is never challenged by a battle without being hemmed in God's protection. Your soul has never encountered a problem that the wisdom of your Wonderful Counselor cannot solve.

You have never touched a rose petal that was devoid of God's glory. You have never tasted a morsel that was empty of God's provision.

You have never known a day that lacked God's blessing.

The life God has given you is beautiful.

Your every prayer rises up before a God who is worthy.

The might of creation, the hope of the ages, the fount of blessing, the everlasting arms, the fortress that guards you: He is worthy.

Your manna in the wilderness, your Balm of Gilead, your Wonderful Counselor, your breakthrough, your Father, and your peace: He is worthy.

He is here, greater than the darkness that surrounds you, vaster than the malevolence that grinds you. He is in your midst, mighty to save you.

He who has overcome death has your life in His hand. He has taken away the judgments against you (Zeph. 3:15).

Your joy for God may be interrupted by suffering. But the Father's joy over you remains uninterrupted. He rejoices that you are in the world. His heart is forever bound to yours even when your heart detaches from His.

He is beautiful. His presence makes life beautiful.

Don't forget to enjoy the beauty of your life. Don't let anxiety or discouragement rob you of who God is, and who you are in Him.

Take time to anchor your heart to God's mighty promises. Work on removing the internal obstacles that block your rest.

Rest in the wonder of God's beauty at work in your life. Quiet your heart in His loving presence.

It's been an honor to walk through this journey with you. I pray you will know that you are not alone. The Father is with you. Hold fast to Him and let Him give you a rested soul.

LINGER

Have I lost sight of the fact that my life is a beautiful gift from God?

PRAYER

God, You are my help. You are my portion and my joy. Your blessings overtake me. Your glory quiets me. Your grace washes away the judgments against me. Thank You for the gift of life. Thank You that You make life beautiful. Help me remember life is beautiful.

OASIS

Jesus, will You make everything beautiful? ~ Ecclesiastes 3:11

REST

He has made everything beautiful in its time.

ECCLESIASTES 3:11

Jesus, I rest knowing that You will make even this season beautiful in its time.

ACKNOWLEDGMENTS

First, thank you, dear reader, for choosing to spend time in this book as you pursue Jesus' rest for your soul. I hope my experience of what has been, until now, a deeply private journey, proves helpful on your own path to peace.

I am indebted to Moody Publishers for making room on their shelves for *The Rested Soul*. I didn't think my quirky concept of bringing together deep meditations and personal photos would find a home anywhere. I am so grateful that Moody took a chance on me and my crazy idea.

I want to offer my sincere gratitude to Judy Dunagan and Pam Pugh for believing in, and supporting this project from the first day, and for making this a better book with their invaluable input. My thanks also to the brilliant team who turned *The Rested Soul* into the beautiful book you are holding: Connor Sterchi; Matt Smartt; and Erik Peterson (to whom we owe the gorgeous cover). This book would not have been possible without your efforts, talent, and grace.

A special thanks to my marvelous agent, Wendy Lawton, and my dear friend Robin Jones Gunn, whose insightful suggestions and warm encouragement helped point me in the right direction for this project.

There would be no book without my hubby. His love, encouragement, and of course, stunning photography bring life and beauty to my inadequate words.

I am filled with gratitude to God, who has brought me so far and held me close through many valleys. I pray He will use these meditations to quiet your own heart and wrap your anxious soul in His peace.

If you are interested in reading more devotionals by me, please sign up for my free monthly newsletter at TessaAfshar.com.

ENTER THE STORY OF RUTH LIKE NEVER BEFORE THROUGH THIS 6-WEEK BIBLE STUDY

MOODY
Publishers®

From the Word to Life®

The story of Ruth is a remarkable tale of bravery, calling, and provision. Join Tessa Afshar in this six-week study and learn how to draw on the same strength and courage that Ruth did and accept God's invitation to new beginnings in your own life.

DVD companion and eBook also available

CAN A CANAANITE HARLOT WHO MADE HER LIVING ENTICING MEN BE A FITTING WIFE FOR A LEADER OF ISRAEL? SHOCKINGLY, THE BIBLE'S ANSWER IS YES.

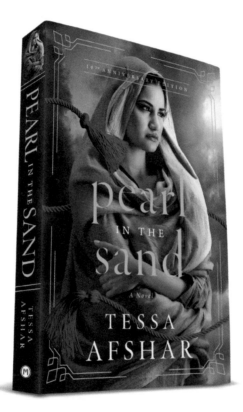

MOODY Publishers®

From the Word to Life®

This 10th anniversary edition of *Pearl in the Sand* includes new features that will invite you into the untold story of Rahab's journey from lowly outcast to redeemed child of God. Through the heartaches of a stormy relationship, Rahab and Salmone learn the true source of one another's worth and find healing in God.

Also available as an eBook